DREAM SEED

God's Blueprint Within You

Clarence Dalrymple

Dream Seed: God's Blueprint Within You

Cover Design and Art Work by Rev. Mary Barratt

Scripture references and quotations have been used by the following versions of the Bible: King James Version of the Holy Bible, The New King James Version, Thomas Nelson Publishers, Nashville, TN, 1999 The Amplified Bible, Zondervan Bible Publishers, Grand Rapids, Michigan, 1965, The Message New Testament With Psalms And Proverbs, Eugene H. Peterson, NAVPRESS Colorado Springs, Colorado 1995, The NIV Study Bible, New International Version, Kenneth L. Barker, general editor, Zondervan Publishers, Grand Rapids, Michigan, 1985, New Living Translation (NLT), Kenneth Taylor, general editor, Tyndale House Publishers, Wheaton, Illinois, 1996.

ISBN-13: 978-1495328572
ISBN-10: 1495328570

Printed in the United States of America

Library of Congress data is available for this title.

Codex Spiritualis Press
http://codexspiritualis.weebly.com

DEDICATIONS

First and foremost, I dedicate this book to the Lord and Savior of my life, Jesus Christ. Your faithfulness has been so great and constant in my life. You have guided each step of my life. You have upheld me and kept me through all my years of serving you. Forever Yours!

I dedicate this book to my wife, Carol Dalrymple, who has gone to be with the Lord. She prophesied before her death that the books in my spirit would come forth.

I dedicate this book to my daughter, Stacey, and her husband, Vance Rogers, who have always encouraged me to do what was in my heart.

I dedicate this book to my granddaughters. I know there is already a strong faith in each of you. The purpose and plan of God will be fulfilled in your lives.

I dedicate this book to Jeanne E. Little. You were chosen by God to be a vital part of Living Faith Ministries International, Inc. You encouraged me and were an instrument in awakening my dream and vision in my heart. Without you, this project would not have happened. Thank you!

I thank God every day for the mentors that He brought into my life. Each one had a special influence on my calling that God had given me. They all recognized that I was created to do something in my life. Even with all my inadequacies and my timid spirit, they were not discouraged from imparting into my life the truths that would eventually become a revelation branded in my spirit.

ACKNOWLEDGMENTS

God puts people in your life to influence your destiny. They are true friends who encourage you and see your heart and vision. I want to extend my personal and sincere thanks to:

Dr. Ron Smith – Thank you for being obedient to the Holy Spirit in October of 1968. You uttered a prophecy concerning the ministry God prepared for me. You have spoken into my life every year since that night. Thank you for being a true mentor and friend.

Pastor John and Dodie Osteen (Lakewood Church, Houston, TX) – Pastor John Osteen, who is now with the Lord, and his wife, Dodie, helped bring me from tradition into the walk of the Spirit and the walk of faith. The years that God allowed me to work with them as associate pastor were the formative years of my ministry today.

Pastor Henry and Naomi Sanders (Faith Outreach Christian Center, Navasota, TX) – You have been true friends since we met in college in 1966. Thank you for your spiritual support during my tough times as well as my good times. You are true friends.

Pastor Philip and Dianne Thurmond (Reigning Love Christian Center, Pittsfield, MA,) – I am grateful that God brought you into my life in 1974. You have encouraged me and supported me in all that God has instructed me to do. You are true friends.

Pastor Malcolm and Sulynn Burton (Northgate Family Church, Spring, TX) – You have been true friends to me and the ministry. You have inspired me to go forward.

Bishop Curtis Baker (Visionaries International, Inc.) – You are an inspiration to me. I am thankful to be able to network with you and your vision. Thank you for your friendship and support.

Dr. Gerald Davis (Overflowing Cup Ministries International, Inc., Conroe, TX) – You and your family have loved me as one of your own. Your life and faith have inspired me to reach out and do what God has ordained in my life.

I want to express my thanks to the many other pastors around the country who have loved me and encouraged me to do God's will for my life. We are all family and are networking together.

Table of Contents

FOREWORD

Lifelong friendships are not only rare; they also produce a three-fold cord that is unbreakable. When fellowship consists of trust, respect, and integrity, this combination enables people to survive all insurmountable odds, achieve exciting goals, and meet all assignments for our wonderful Lord and Savior.

Clarence Dalrymple is a true champion and an awesome contender of the faith. Satan's crucibles (and there have been many) have only served to refine his God-given credentials that have now promoted him into the apostolic order. Clarence has experience in all five gift-offices and is one of the few ministers whom I know that excels as apostle, prophet, evangelist, pastor, and teacher. Shortly after his precious wife, Carol, was promoted to Heaven, I saw the mantle of the Apostle and the apostolic anointing draped upon "C."

I remember when the Lord used us to give "C" a prophecy. It was at St. Paul's Assembly of God Church on Grannis Street in Houston, Texas. "C" was only eighteen years of age at this time. He believed it! He embraced it! He never turned loose of it. He bubbled with joy just talking about it. Today, some forty-five years later, the prophecy is "hastening to fulfillment." Included in the prophecy was the phrase: "I will put wings on your shoes. You will ascend into many nations, especially, Great Britain." This is now happening.

"C," as I call him, is also a visionary. That is why this book, The Dream Seed, God's Blueprint Within You, is a must-read.

I trust that you, dear readers, not only enjoy the contents of this book, but in doing so, become aware, as I have, that the author is a man sent by God to bless this generation in a way only he can.

Dr. Ronald G. Smith, D.D.
Independence, Missouri

INTRODUCTION

Universal Questions

The universal questions that tug at the heart of every individual are: What is my purpose in life? Why was I born? How can I know the divine purpose that God has for me?

I am sure that if you are honest with yourself, you will admit that these questions have come to your mind often. Deep within all persons is a connection to the Creator of our being. The link to God was planted deep in our spirit before we were conceived. God preprogrammed His blueprint for our lives before we ever arrived on planet Earth. When the Lord spoke to Jeremiah, as a young prophet, He said to him, "Before I formed you in the belly I knew you; and before you came forth out of the womb I sanctified you, and I ordained you a prophet unto the nations" (Jer. 1:4-5 NKJV). What was true for Jeremiah is also true for each of us.

I have been in Christian ministry for over four decades. I have observed people of all occupations and lifestyles. Many have discovered their purpose in life. I have seen a sparkle in their eyes as they accomplished the assignment God had given them. Their joy level was high as they did what they were put on Earth to do.

On the other hand, many I know have yet to discover their divine purpose. They live in what I call a "survival mode" because they cannot see beyond their present circumstances and are enslaved to an unfulfilling life. Instead of that sparkle of hope in their eyes, sadness and hopelessness are all I see. If the eyes are truly the windows of the soul, then these eyes speak of emptiness therein.

I love people. My sincere desire is to touch lives with a word from God that will enable Christian men and women to rise up in faith and begin the exciting journey God has already mapped out for them. The purpose for this book is to help every person to find his or her pre-ordained, divinely created destiny and purpose.

My desire is to encourage you that the best is yet to come. It does not matter if your dream and vision has been dormant for years. It is never too late to begin to fulfill what God has placed in you. God will accelerate that vision, restore those dormant years, and enable you fulfill His divine purpose and call.

There *is* a special plan for your life. There *is* a dream being birthed in *you*. Others have opinions, but you have direction. Allow God to define the plan He has designed for you. God is saying, look again at your dreams, and see them from the present. When you originally dreamed them, you had only some of the pieces. Now is the time to take another look. Declare along with the psalmist, "The Lord will work out His plans for my life" (Ps. 138:8 NLT).

I am praying for you and each one who reads this book. I pray that God will show you plainly His design for your life.

I pray that you will have the boldness and courage to begin this new journey. I pray that you will find contentment and joy in knowing that you have fulfilled the perfect will of God for your life.

Clarence Dalrymple
2011

Today is the first day of the rest of your life.

CHAPTER ONE

A BLUEPRINT FOR YOUR LIFE

"You are God's Masterpiece with a 'DREAM SEED'

Planted in your spirit by God."

CHAPTER ONE

A BLUEPRINT FOR YOUR LIFE

"Hope deferred makes the heart sick, but when
the desire comes it is a tree of life."
– Proverbs.13:12 NKJV

You did not just "happen." You are not an accident of nature. Before you were formed in your mother's womb, God had designed the blueprint for your life. He knew the generation that you would be born in and had a special job, a purpose, in mind just for you.

God's plan is not just some haphazard scheme that He threw together at the last minute. His plan is a Master Blueprint, designed for each person in every situation on the face of the earth. God has orchestrated a course for every individual that, if accepted, will bring glory and honor to His kingdom. God knows the beginning and the ending. He is the all-knowing Creator.

Just look around you. The creation of the universe did not just flit across God's mind one day. He is a God of precision and detail. He knew exactly what He desired and created this universe for a specific purpose. The moon and the sun both have a purpose. He placed them strategically the right distance from each other and from Earth. Every star is placed in the exact location that He planned. Everything He created works together in perfect harmony.

I know that many people feel like they were born on the wrong side of the tracks and there is no hope of success, or even survival. But where you are born and where you live does not determine whether you are successful. You are the deciding factor. God will make sure that the message of hope gets to you. Then you must decide whether to yield to Him and follow the blueprint that He has designed for just for you.

Isaiah, one of Israel's greatest prophets, had been dead for seventy years. Jerusalem was falling to the enemy and was being trodden down by the destructive forces of evil assigned to her. But God had chosen another prophet to rise up and take the responsibility of fulfilling the divine will of God. Jeremiah was that person.

Jeremiah was a priest in the tribe of Benjamin. God had called him before he was ever formed in his mother's womb, had sanctified him, and called him to be a prophet to the nations.

"Then the word of the Lord came unto me, saying, Before I formed you in the belly I knew you; and before thou came forth out of the womb I sanctified you, and I ordained you a prophet unto the nations." (Jer. 1:4-5 KJV)

God Has a Purpose for Each Individual

The word "purpose" is defined as: "the reason for which something exists," or "the reason for being."

Many people lose hope and lose their vision. Many never find their reason for being. Some even come to that desperate place of giving up because they fail to perceive a future. They cannot see any reason for living. But I want to tell you something: there is a reason for your being. You have a purpose. You have a calling. There is a place for you in God's creation. No one but you can fill it.

"For we are God's masterpiece. He has created us new in Christ Jesus, so that we can do the good things He planned for us long ago" (Eph. 2:1 NLT).

God has a Master Plan—a plan uniquely designed for every person in every situation. You might feel your life is more of a mess than a masterpiece. You need to begin to see yourself as God sees you—a son or daughter fulfilling His plan.

I want to share with you a story of an extraordinary person who discovered her God-designed blueprint.

A woman married during World War II and had a family. Her husband came home from the war and divorced her. She was all alone with her children, but she knew God, and she knew the lordship of Jesus Christ.

She began to work and support herself. She did not have any type of professional training. One day she was at a direct sales company, sitting in the back row. It was Stanley Home Products. She had worked for three weeks, and had averaged only seven dollars per week. She was hurting.

She watched a woman march up on that stage and be crowned Queen for the year for selling the most Stanley Home Products. Our single mom said to herself, "I'm going to do that! I'm going to do it!"

The following year the crown was placed upon her

head. It was not a big deal to anyone else. Who cares about being queen for Stanley Home Products? But it was big to her. She had accomplished a goal that she set for herself. Her destiny for her life began to unfold, and she realized she was a person of significance to God.

That woman was Mary Kay Ashe, the founder of Mary Kay Cosmetics. Her company became one of the largest cosmetic companies in the world, doing over $300 million worth of business annually, with over 200,000 independent women working with and for her.

The start of Mary Kay cosmetics was fueled by her determination to give other women the opportunity she felt she had always been denied. She wanted to give women the opportunity to go as far as their abilities could take them; to be the very best they could be. She wanted to give women a chance to realize they are wonderful and special, and that they can succeed beyond their wildest dreams, if they are just given the opportunity. So many have accomplished so much. So what was once her dream has now become a wonderful reality.

Maybe you are also "sitting in the back row" and hurting. Maybe your heart is sick because you have not seen your dream come to pass. Don't despair! God has the inspired plan. He has the blueprint for your life.

A person without hope is one who lives with no purpose and feels as if there is no exit to his situation. When hope is gone, all is gone; nothing is left. To the person with hope, difficulties are only opportunities for God to show His power. HOPE NEVER SAYS FAIL!

When the desire or dream comes, it is like a tree of life. There is nothing more rewarding than seeing a plan come to pass and a dream seed that has been conceived by the Holy Spirit in your heart being birthed.

God Will Work With Your Dream

God has purpose for you and wants you to see that purpose. At the new birth, we are transferred into the Kingdom of God. We are no longer subject to Satan and the influences of this world. When we willingly submit to Jesus Christ, our thoughts and actions are going to please Him. Before we were born again, our mind was alienated from the things of God. Our mind was an enemy to God and the good things that He has for us. But after receiving Christ's salvation, we are reconciled to God and "delivered" from the power of darkness. This expression, power of darkness, suggests the idea of disorder. God has brought us out of the state of confusion and the control of the negative influences in our world. We have been "translated" (transferred, moved from one place to another) into the Kingdom of the Son of God. Here, another language is spoken. Our mind is ready to be filled with the thoughts of God and His promises. We are no longer subject to being conformed and fashioned after this world and its environment.

"We are in this world, but not of this world."

God's desire is to let His divine purpose work in you. God wants you to prosper. He delights in the prosperity of

His servants. God is more excited for His blueprint for your life to be fulfilled than you are.

We must think God's thoughts, and talk like God talks. We are to act like God. We can and must do big things. Know that God has a plan. He has a dream.

"But you shall remember the Lord your God: for it is he that gives you power [ability] to get wealth that he may establish his covenant which he swore to your fathers, as it is this day." (Deut. 8:18 KJV)

"Let them shout for joy, and be glad, that favor my righteous cause: yea, let them say continually, Let the Lord be magnified, which takes pleasure in the prosperity of his servant." (Ps. 35:27 KJV)

Your Circumstances Do Not Dictate Your Future.

God has always been in the creation business. He will take your life of nothing and make it a productive life to bring glory to God.

Man was created in the image of God. He was given authority in the earth and over every created thing in the earth.

"And God said, Let Us Father, Son, and Holy Spirit make mankind in Our image, after Our likeness; and let them have complete authority over the fish of the sea. The birds of the air, the tame beasts, and over all of the earth, and over everything that creeps upon the earth." (Gen. 1:26 AMP)

Adam was to have authority over circumstances. He was to have authority over adversities. He was to subdue the earth, "to tend and guard and keep it" (Gen. 2:15 AMP). He was to cause the earth to yield its fruit. He was to succeed. But Satan, the intruder, came uninvited into the arena where Adam ruled. Satan came tempting, testing, and trying to talk them into rebellion and disobedience, to fall just like he did in the beginning of time. As long as Adam and Eve would stay obedient to the blueprint and plan, there would be no problem. As long as they walked in obedience, they would have life. Obedience releases the mercy of God in our lives. Disobedience causes us to walk though life with no covering of mercy.

Man began to live and be led by the natural senses. Their spiritual lamp, the light, which gave the ability to see beyond the natural realm, had gone out. They could not see beyond their physical senses. "To be carnally minded is death" (Rom. 8:6 KJV). To be carnally minded means to be sense-minded, or to think according to your senses. This is the reason that people who have a dream given by God respond by saying: "no way that I can do that."

Carnally minded man is enslaved to his surroundings. His dreams and visions are limited. The only thing the enslaved man can see is sickness and disease. He can only see fear and failure.

On the other hand, those who are spiritually minded can do all things. To be spiritually minded is life. This is the law of abundance. Spiritually minded people do not see lack. All they see is abundance.

A spiritually minded person sees: **I can make it.**

A spiritually minded person sees: **I can do it.**

A spiritually minded person sees: **I can overcome.**

Dr. T.L. Osborn said, "That's what God created us for —life; abundant life, as we operate in the "Laws of Life."

"For the law of the Spirit of life in Christ Jesus made me free from the law of sin and of death." (Rom. 8:2 KJV)

God's plan is a blueprint for man. A blueprint is a plan for the future. As you begin to see God's will and walk in the path that He has designed, you will begin to see your destiny unfold.

Remember, there is a "dream seed" planted in your spirit by God your creator. Give God the opportunity to work in you to define the purpose that He has uniquely designed for your life.

YOU ARE GOD'S MASTERPIECE WITH A "DREAM SEED" PLANTED IN YOUR SPIRIT BY GOD.

CHAPTER TWO

THE BIRTHING OF YOUR DREAMS

"The seed that God planted in each of us is ready to be birthed and to produce the results that He desires."

CHAPTER 2

THE BIRTHING OF YOUR DREAMS

"And God said, Let the earth bring forth grass, the herb yielding seed, and the fruit tree yielding fruit after his kind, whose seed is in itself, upon the earth: and it was so."
– Genesis 1:11 NKJV

God is the creator of this earth. There is an order to everything that He created. Seedtime and harvest time are divine parts of God's orderly plan. As long as the earth remains, there will always be seedtime and harvest time. God ordained each seed to birth and produce after its kind. That is God's law. Inside every seed is a perfect plan for its reproduction. Seeds are plant structures formed in the cones or flowers of plants. Once the female part of the plant is fertilized with the pollen produced by the male part of plant, a seed is formed. Although most seeds are very small, they are capable of growing into new plants, as great as a giant redwood tree, or as prolific as a zucchini vine. Seeds may remain inactive for weeks, months, or even years, lying in wait for growing conditions to be just right for sprouting. When the temperature is favorable and the water supply is adequate, the seeds become active and quickly begin to sprout and grow.

Seeds come in a wide variety of shapes, colors, and sizes. Many of them are edible, such as sunflower seeds, pinto beans, corn, and peas. Seeds contain stored food, intended to nourish the new plant as it begins to grow. This food, rich in proteins and carbohydrates, are a source of nutrients for animals and humans. In fact, seeds provide most of the people of the world with their staple foods—wheat, corn, and rice.

God has Placed Seeds of Greatness in Each One of Us

God placed His plan in each one of us in seed form. Every individual has been created by God and has special gifts and talents put there by Him designed to benefit His Kingdom.

"Having then gifts differing according to the grace [ability] that is given to us, let us use them." (Rom. 12:6 NKJV)

We are all wonderfully created by God, and each one of us possesses unique qualities. If every person looked and behaved the same, this would be a boring world. But we all have different gifts according to the grace that is given to us. The word "grace" is the same word used in the Greek language (*charis*) meaning "ability." In other words, God has given each person a unique ability or calling, and He also gives the divine ability to perform that calling.

For you formed my inward parts. You covered me in my mother's womb. I will praise You, for I am fearfully and wonderfully made. Marvelous are Your works, and that my soul knows very well. My frame was not hidden from You when I was made in secret, and skillfully wrought in the lowest parts of the earth. Your eyes saw my substance, being yet unformed. And in Your book they all were written. The

days fashioned for me, when as yet there were none of them. How precious also are Your thoughts to me, O God! How great is the sum of them! If I should count them, they would be more in number than the sand; when I awake, I am still with You. (Ps. 139:13-18 NKJV)

The seed that God planted in each of us is ready to be birthed and to produce the desired results that He desires. But, just as the seeds of plants and trees may remain inactive for weeks, months, and sometimes years, lying in wait for growing conditions to be just right for sprouting, the "seed" that God has conceived in your spirit by the Holy Spirit will come alive and develop and sprout when the conditions are right.

Some of us discovered our God-designed "seed" after many years. Some of our lives went opposite directions from God's plan for us. It is like being on an interstate highway with all the different exits. Some take an exit ramp and go off the main road. But because of the mercy of God and His perfect will for our lives, He preserves that "seed." He allows us to re-enter the road to success where the favorable conditions (the Lord's perfect timing) can nurture the seed and prepare it for birthing—the birthing of the "dream seed."

A seed is something that has been preprogrammed. The word "programmed" is defined as something that is alive, recorded, or was alive beforehand. The Greek (*pro gramma*) means "to write beforehand, to make a schedule or plan." A blueprint is like a program, isn't it? Something recorded, something written before. The "seed" inside you has been programmed for a specific assignment. You may attempt to chart your own life, but God, as your creator, has a specific purpose for your life. It has been pre-ordained before you were ever born. Nothing else will produce the spiritual joy that comes when we discover our divinely appointed purpose.

"And I will put enmity between you and the woman, and between your seed and her seed: he shall bruise your head, and you shall bruise his heel." (Gen. 3:15 NKJV)

God prophesied about the "seed" of the woman that would eventually defeat Satan and his scheme to bring every man and woman under his evil dominion. God spoke to the serpent in the Garden of Eden after Adam and Eve had yielded to its temptation. God told the serpent that the "seed" of the woman would bruise his head.

It took four thousand years and hundreds of generations for the "seed" of the woman to be born. But a young maiden named Mary found favor with God. He chose her to be overshadowed by the Holy Spirit and conceive the supernatural seed that would one day redeem and restore fallen humankind back to its position as sons of God. (See Luke 1:26-35.)

"But when the fullness of the time came, God sent forth his Son, born of a woman, born under the law, that he might redeem them that were under the law, that we might receive the adoption of sons. And because you are sons, God sent forth the Spirit of his Son into our hearts, crying, Abba,

Father." (Gal. 4:4-6 NKJV)

The "seed" of the woman was birthed, and Jesus Christ was that baby in the manger. He began to grow in knowledge and the wisdom of God, His Father. He was found at the age of twelve expounding the Scriptures in the temple to all the scribes. At the age of thirty, His cousin, John the Baptist, who was the forerunner of the earthly ministry of Jesus Christ, baptized him in the Jordan River. Three–and-one-half years later, this "seed" of the woman was crucified on the cross, was buried, and rose again on the third day according to the prophecies. Through His death, the harvest of all those who believe was brought into the Kingdom of God.

God placed His perfect redemption plan into seed form, sometimes called the "incorruptible seed." Inside every other seed is a perfect plan for the reproduction of itself—a perfect blueprint.

A blueprint is a plan for the future. God put His blueprint, His plan, into a seed. Jesus Christ the Son of God is that seed. Jesus Christ, the Son of God, fulfilled the divine plan of God. God has also planted within each of our hearts a similar seed, the unique purpose of God for our lives. When we act upon it, that plan will begin to unfold.

Your dream and your vision and the plan God has for you is like a seed. That seed can just lie there and never release what is on the inside of it. But if you allow that seed to be birthed and grow, you will see the desired results that God intended for your life.

Everything created contains instructions and an

assignment. Instructions may be unknown, ignored, or distorted, but they do exist. Each seed has a divine instruction to produce. God has placed within all of us a desire and a command to increase, produce, and multiply. Within you are an invisible calling, purpose, and destiny.

An oak tree begins with just a small acorn. It looks inadequate to produce a towering strong oak tree. But the power inside the seed is what makes the difference.

That small seed inside your spirit may seem as though nothing will ever come of it. But God has instructed us not to look at things as ordinary, but to see, by faith, the finished product. God looks into the future and sees the finished product. God delights to use those who are inferior to others and feel inadequate of seeing great things done for the Kingdom of God. God knows that a humble spirit will allow His resurrection power to explode and produce a "giant" for God.

Never underestimate the power of God and His ability to create and enable the weakest individual to become the strongest.

There is no such thing as "the wrong side of the tracks" with our God. We all have our Father's attributes in our spirit. God has confidence in you. You are created in His likeness. God made you, and He has programmed you for victory.

God will work where there is an attitude of faith. God has always taken ordinary people and made them extraordinary individuals. You are special to God. He loves you with an everlasting love. His desire is to protect, preserve, and provide supernaturally for you. You are not alone, because He has promised never to leave you alone or in a lurch. He has also garrisoned angels about you to minister to you and for you as an heir of salvation. "Are they not all ministering spirits, sent forth to minister for them who shall be heirs of salvation?" (Heb. 1:14 NKJV).

Be encouraged, because that "seed" that God has planted in your spirit is getting ready to sprout and grow for the glory of God. You do not have to be a prisoner of your circumstances. God has provided an escape route for you—through accepting the victory that Christ won for us with His blood, defeating Satan forever.

You have been delivered from the power of Satan and transferred into the Kingdom of God where Jesus Christ reigns as Lord over all. You are now free to become a creator of your future.

You do not have to be a prisoner of your circumstances.

CHAPTER THREE

THE REALITY OF YOUR VISION

"We determine how much of the vision will be fulfilled by our obedience and actions of faith."

CHAPTER 3

THE REALITY OF YOUR VISION

"Where there is no vision [no redemptive revelation of God] the people perish; but he who keeps the law [of God, which includes that of man] blessed, happy, fortunate [and enviable] is he."
– Proverbs 29:18 AMP

Every human being on planet Earth asks:
What is my purpose in life?
Why was I born?
Why am I here?
What am I supposed to be doing?

For a number of years, I also wondered what my purpose was. Many people have many interests and have the ability to do many things. But they die unfulfilled, never discovering their life's assignment.

That's right—you do not decide your assignment, you discover it. Your assignment is something you alone must discern. God may bring people into your life who recognize the gifts that are inside of you. They may even speak prophetically to you, revealing exactly what God is saying and doing. But you have to ultimately discern the divine vision and dream that God wants to birth inside you. In order to be able to discern that divine vision, a relationship with God is absolutely necessary. "So then every one of us shall give account of himself to God" (Rom. 14:12 NKJV).

You are here on Earth for a specific assignment that God has given you gifts for, according to your purpose. "But unto every one of us is given grace [ability] according to the measure of the gift of Christ" (Eph. 4:7 NKJV). God's grace [ability] is adequate for the particular calling or gift of Christ that is already in you.

Knowing Your Purpose in Life

The word "purpose" is defined as the reason for which something exists, or the reason for being. Many people lose hope and lose their vision before their purpose in life is revealed to them. Some even attempt suicide, and some succeed, because the enemy of their souls convinces them they are worthless and have no reason for existence.

But let me tell you the truth. There *is* a reason for your being. You have a purpose. You have a calling. There is a place for you in God's divine plan. No one but you can fulfill that vision.

God Will Give You Direction with Purpose

You will accomplish that vision and dream because you will know where you are going. You will have direction with purpose. "But there is a spirit in man: and the inspiration of the Almighty gives them understanding" (Job 32:8 KJV).

This is the key to your vision. This is the key to your future. When you can see the dream, and therefore have hope and a reason for living, you will have action with purpose. You *must* have action with purpose. "Any enterprise is built by wise planning. It becomes strong through common sense, and profits wonderfully by keeping abreast of the facts" (Prov. 24:3 TLB).

That dream and that vision are birthed within you as an invisible picture of your future and purpose on Earth. God is very detailed in everything He does. He has explicit instructions for you to follow as you fulfill His purpose for your life.

Satan will always develop a strategy to cloud this picture and paralyze the vision and dream that God is birthing in you. Satan's job is to interfere and to influence you to abandon this purpose, so you will never see your destiny fulfilled.

Give birth to your vision and dreams. Do not let them die inside you to carry to the grave. Someone so notably stated, "The wealthiest piece of real estate is the cemetery. In each of those graves are treasures beyond our imaginations. Inside those coffins are unpublished books, unpublished songs, businesses that never got started, and unfulfilled relationships that never developed, because the person lying there failed to 'see' what God had planned for them."

"Hope deferred makes the heart sick: but when the desire comes, it is a tree of life." (Prov. 13:12 NKVJ)

God Wants Us to See the Whole Picture as He Sees it.

Helen Keller was asked, "What would be worse than being born blind?" She replied, "To have sight without vision!"

Let's look at four levels of vision that people demonstrate:

1. Some people never see it. They are *Wanderers*. They drift aimlessly in life, never seeing the purpose and plan that God has designed for them. They never have the satisfaction of having a dream fulfilled.

2. Some people see it but never pursue it. They are *Followers*. These individuals never develop their full potential. They stay at the same level of growth for years and years. Usually, they allow fear to dominate their minds, which hinders them from moving into the realm of achievement.

3. Some people see it and pursue it. They are *Achievers*. They do not allow the negative forces in life to stop them from moving forward. They live lives of satisfaction, knowing that they have achieved their dreams.

4. Some people see it, pursue it, and help others see it. They are *Leaders*. Not only do they see the entire picture, they are also able to convey the message to others so they too can rise up and accomplish the dream God has designed.

Vision vs. Revelation

A vision is a mental image. It is the "dream seed" in the heart. It is foreseeing the future. A vision is understanding, enlightenment, and illuminated truth. Unless there is a vision, you will have no direction in life. Vision is looking ahead over the horizon. Hope believes with that confident expectation, it will happen. Vision has purpose. Vision is seeing beyond the natural realm.

"For he endured as seeing Him who is invisible." (Heb. 11:27 NKJV)

"I pray that the God of our Lord Jesus Christ, the Father of Glory, may give unto you the spirit of wisdom and revelation in the knowledge of Him." (Eph. 1:17 NKJV)

Revelation is defined: "to take off the cover, to disclose, and to reveal." It is the insight into God's plan. Revelation is a Spirit-taught truth.

Any Revelation is Connected with the Word of God.

Whether it is by dreams, visions, or the enlightenment of the Word, revelation concerns the promises of God and their fulfillment in your life.

"As His divine power has given to us all things that pertain to life and godliness, through the knowledge of Him who called us by glory and virtue. By which have been given to us exceedingly great and precious promises, that through these you may be partakers of the divine nature, having escaped the corruption that is in the world through lust." (1 Pet. 1:3-4 NKJV)

God has made provisions for you to be able to see the "vision" and make it plain to your understanding:

1. **You need to see the vision.** The Holy Spirit will reveal the purpose and plan of God for your life. He will become that spirit of wisdom and revelation to you, allowing your spirit to be enlightened and to know the hope of His

calling in you.

"But there is a spirit in man: and the inspiration of the Almighty gives them understanding." (Job 32:8 KJV)

"That the God of our Lord Jesus Christ, the Father of glory, may give unto you the spirit of wisdom and revelation in the knowledge of him: The eyes of your understanding being enlightened; that ye may know what is the hope of his calling, and what the riches of the glory of his inheritance in the saints." (Eph. 1:17-18 NKJV)

2. **You need to receive the vision**. God is revealing His purpose and gifts in your life. Now you know what you are born for. But the final decision rests with you. You have to decide to say yes, I will do it. King Agrippa was *almost* persuaded to say yes to God and begin a new life with purpose and meaning. But he did not do it. (See Acts 26:28.)

3. **You need to obey the vision.** It is one thing to know what God's plan and purpose is, but an entirely different thing to submit—to obey with the intent to please God. "Roll your works upon the Lord. Commit and trust them wholly to Him. He will cause your thoughts to become agreeable to His will, and so shall your plans be established and succeed" (Prov. 16:3 AMP).

4. **You need to expand the vision.** Paul, the apostle, had a divine encounter with Christ one day. He was on the road

to Damascus with papers of ordinances against the Christians and leaders in that region. On that road, he received a revelation of Jesus Christ and realized his purpose in life was not to kill Christians, but to preach the Gospel and see the world come to Christ. God appeared to Paul for a purpose. It was to allow Paul to see himself like God saw him, a minister to the world. He was to convince the world that Jesus Christ is alive and able to deliver it from destruction. He was to pray for their eyes to be opened as his were. He was to turn them from Satan to God. Like Paul, our gifts and vision are not for our selfish gain, but serve a far more important role in serving others.

Vision Sees as God Sees

Joshua had to see with eyes of faith and perceive the future that God had for the children of Israel. He had taken command and become the leader of Israel after Moses died. God spoke to Joshua and assured him that just as He was with Moses, He would also be with him. In fact, God reaffirmed the promised boundaries of the land that He had established from the beginning. The challenge to march forward and possess the land was issued thusly: "Every place the sole of your foot treads belongs to you." This was what God proclaimed.

> ***We determine how much of the vision will be fulfilled by our obedience and actions of faith.***

Many start out obeying the vision that is in their heart.

The "dream seed" is birthed and the developmental process is underway. God has drawn a vivid picture, and the future seems clear. These folks rejoice over the discovery of their purpose.

But then the first giant obstacle stands in the middle of the path. Just like Joshua when he encountered the first hindrance to the progress of Israel possessing the land that God had given them, discouragement sets in. God never said there would not be challenges. In fact, the report of the spies related that there were "giants" in the land. The report showed that there were alien armies that controlled the territory. Joshua had an encounter with the "Angel of the Lord" in Joshua chapter 5. He asked the Angel of the Lord: "Are you with us or against us?" The Angel said, "I am the Captain of The Host of The Lord. Take off your shoe, for the place you are standing is holy." And Joshua humbled himself and obeyed.

Crisis always occurs at the curve of change.

Each time we take a step towards the goal, opposition will surely be there. Jericho was the first walled city that stood before Joshua and Israel. Jericho was secured by high walls and well defended.

God told Joshua ... "See! I have given Jericho into your hand, its king, and the mighty men of valor" (Josh. 6:2 NKJV). This is the past present perfect tense of this verb-I have given. It means I have already given the city (past tense) and it is yours now (present perfect tense). Joshua was able to lead the children of Israel to victory over Jericho when he could see as God sees.

See, (like God sees) I have given (past, present, perfect tense.) It is yours for the taking.

Abraham Had to Perceive What God Perceived

Abraham had believed for Isaac, the son God had promised him. He was getting old, yet he believed God. Sarah, his wife, made the suggestion to take Hagar, her maid servant from Egypt, and conceive a child with her. Abraham consented, believing that God's promise would be fulfilled that way. He never took into consideration the consequences of his action. But God saw his faith, and at the ripe old age of one hundred, God did the supernatural. Isaac, the promised son, was born.

But God required one last test of his commitment to the covenant. He required him to sacrifice Isaac on the altar. Abraham had confidence in the faithfulness of God. In fact, he told his servants to wait while he and Isaac went to the mountain, about a three days journey, and worshipped the Lord. And then they would return.

On the way up the mountain, Isaac pondered in his heart the thing that he and his father, Abraham, were doing. He had learned from his father the meaning of sacrifices. He knew the things that were required in order to worship God. He saw that they had the wood which was needed to build the altar, and the ropes that were needed to tie down the sacrifice were there and available. Isaac was not a mere child as some Bible story books portray; he was a grown man. Many historians have determined that Isaac was around thirty to thirty-three years of age. He had sacrificed many animals upon the altar with Abraham. Therefore, Isaac asked a legitimate question, "Where is the sacrifice?" Abraham said, "God will provide himself a sacrifice." Jehovah Jirah—God will provide. The original Hebrew of the word "provide" suggests "seeing as God sees." God knew the ram was waiting there.

Abraham was obedient to God concerning offering Isaac. He knew that God had supernaturally fulfilled the vision in allowing Isaac to be born to him and Sara in their mature years. Abraham had faith that God, who promised the seed and fulfilled His promise of allowing the seed (Isaac) to be born, would also watch over His promise by providing the sacrifice of raising Isaac from the dead, if necessary, to fulfill the vision.

"By faith Abraham, when he was tried, offered up Isaac: and he that had received the promises offered up his only begotten son, of whom it was said, That in Isaac shall your seed be called: accounting that God was able to raise him up, even from the dead; from whence also he received him in a figure." (Heb. 11:17-19 KJV)

There are three things that you need to do to see the fulfillment of your dream:

1. You have to see the *invisible*. You have to look beyond the natural realm and see God and the end results of your

dream. "He indeed was foreordained before the foundation of the world, but was manifest in these last times for you" (1 Pet. 1:20 NKJV).

2. You have to choose the *imperishable* over the perishable. The choice you make is for eternal things. George Mueller had a children's home in England. Every day was a "Miracle Day." He chose to serve God by helping these children to see a loving Father. These young lives were impacted by the daily miracles of provision and care they received. Only eternity will reveal the results of one man choosing the imperishable.

3. You have to learn to do the *impossible*. When you see beyond the natural realm, you can take the "Giant Leap of Faith" and see God perform, supernaturally, the promises to fulfill your dreams.

God's desire is for the best in your life. His purpose and vision and dream that are being birthed in you are His priority. He will complete what he has begun and bring it to fruition in your life.

"For we know that all things are possible to him that believes." (Mark 9:23 NKJV)

"I can do all things through Christ that strengthens me." (Phil. 4:13 KJV)

"I am ready for anything and equal to anything through Christ who infuses His strength into my inner man [that is, I am self sufficient in Christ's sufficiency]." (Phil. 4:13 AMP)

I Am What God Says I Am; I Possess What God Says I Possess;I Can Do What God Says I Can Do.

CHAPTER FOUR

THE BIRTH, DEATH, AND RESURRECTION OF YOUR VISION

"God is faithful not to forget His promise to you. His creative power is still working on your behalf that seed of promise in your spirit will burst forth and produce the intention of its purpose. We have Purpose in this life and God wants it to become reality."

CHAPTER 4

THE BIRTH, DEATH, AND RESURRECTION OF YOUR VISION

"Where there is no vision the people perish."
– Proverbs 29:18 NKJV

The Bible has a lot to say about the visions and dreams of your heart:

"Where there is no vision [no redemptive revelation of God] the people perish; but he who keeps the law [of God, which includes that of man] blessed, happy, fortunate [and enviable] is he." (Prov. 29:18 AMP)

The Birth of Your Vision

Have you ever looked at a flower seed and wondered how something so beautiful could come from such a tiny dry kernel? The birth of vision is like a seed. It does not seem like much in the beginning. The acorn that lies on the ground does not look anything like the giant oak tree that it will become. Similarly, God does not see the seed as the finished product, but as the beginning of something beautiful and great that it will become.

A seed is designed according to the law of increase. Each seed has the resurrection power of the Holy One in it, waiting to erupt. A seed signifies that Jesus is Lord in this earth. Seeds may remain inactive for weeks, months, or even years, lying in wait for growing conditions to be just right for sprouting. When the temperature is favorable and the water supply is adequate, seeds become active and quickly begin to sprout and grow.

Do not give up on the dream seed that is the beginning of your vision. It is designed by God to sprout at exact and perfect time that God has ordained.

The Death of Your Vision

It's good to be passionate about your dream, but did you know a dream could actually become an idol? That happens when you decide you are not going to be happy unless life happens your way. The fact is, sometimes you have to release your dream back to the Father who gave it to you. There comes a time that we have to let go of the dream and put it in God's hands.

Sometimes we can get frustrated because we are trying to force things to happen according to our timetable. Sometimes we hold on to things too tightly. But when we finally are willing to let them go, that's when God can bring them to pass. If you choose to release that frustration and not let it become the center of your attention, but instead, use that same time and energy to thank God that He's directing your steps, then you open the door for God to give you the desires of your heart.

Remember, God already knows what we want and what we need. He's the One who put those desires in us. We shouldn't be consumed by trying to make things happen. Instead, a greater act of faith is to be happy where you are right now. You have to stay open and trust God, because He has good plans in store for your future!

The Resurrection of Your Vision

In the book of 2 Kings chapter 4 is a story of a woman and her husband who had ministered to the prophet Elisha. They built a small chamber in their home so he would have a place to rest when he came through the area.

One day the prophet asked what they wanted God to do for them. The couple desired a son. God honored the request and gave them the desire of their heart. When the boy was in his teens, he was working in the fields with his father. While working, the boywas overcome with the heat and fell dead from heat stroke. But the mother did not panic. She put the boy in the bed in the chamber that she and her husband had built for Elisha. She journeyed to where Elisha was staying. When he saw her coming down the road, Elisha sent his servant to inquire about what was troubling her. The woman replied in faith, "All is well!"

When she reached Elisha, she grabbed his feet, and Gehazi the servant came near to push her away. But Elisha said, "Let her alone; for her soul is in deep distress, and the Lord has hidden it from me, and has not told me" (2 Kings 4:27 NKJV).

She began to cry unto Elisha. "Did I ask a son of my Lord? Did I not say, do not deceive me?" (v. 28). Elisha immediately told Gehazi, "Get yourself ready, and take my staff in your hand, and be on your way, if you meet anyone, do not greet him; and if anyone greets you, do not answer him; but lay my staff on the face of the child" (V.29). And the mother said, "As the Lord lives, and as your soul lives, I will not leave you" (v.30).

Gehazi went ahead and did as the man of God instructed him. But there was no movement from the boy. He ran out on the road to meet Elisha and told him, "The child has not awakened" (v.31).

Elisha came into the house to where the child was lying dead upon his bed. He went in and shut the door behind the two of them, and prayed to the Lord.

Elisha went up and lay on the child, stretching out his body on top of the dead child. He put his mouth on his mouth, his eyes on his eyes, and his hands on his hands. The flesh of the boy became warm. The man of God returned and walked back and forth in the house, and again went up and stretched himself out on him; then the child sneezed seven times, and the child opened his eyes.

Elisha calls for Gehazi and said, "Call this Shunammite woman." So he called her, and when she came into him, he said, "Pick up your son" (v.36). The mother rejoiced, for her son had been raised to life to finish and fulfill his destiny.

When the time comes when it looks like your dream has died—that it is all over with—you have to make the decision to shut yourself up with God. There in His presence, He will give you divine instructions. And according to your faith and God's timing, He will resurrect your dream.

Joseph and his Dream

Joseph was the favorite son of his father, Jacob. His father gave a multi-colored coat to him. The other sons did not receive a gift like this. Jacob's favoritism created sibling rivalry that permeated the lives of his sons.

One night, God gave Joseph a dream. He saw all of his

brother's sheaves of grain bowing to his sheaf of grain. Joseph told his dream to his older brothers. Jealousy arose in them and they schemed to get rid of Joseph. They wanted to kill him, but his brother Rueben intervened and saved Joseph from death. Instead of killing him, they threw him into a pit until they could sell him to a company of Ishmaelites who took him into Egypt. In Egypt, Joseph was sold as a slave. His dream, which he told prematurely, was shattered by all these negative events that transpired. It looked like all of his hope was lost.

Although Joseph ended up in Egypt as a slave, God's favor never left his life. Even though his status had been reduced, God was still with him and promoted him in the time of adversity. He ended up as a slave to Potiphar, an officer of Pharaoh, captain of the guard.

Potiphar saw that the Lord was with Joseph and that the Lord made all that Joseph did to prosper. Joseph found favor in the sight of Potiphar. He served him and then was made overseer of his house, and all that he had was put under his authority. The Lord blessed the Egyptian's house because of Joseph.

Things were going well for Joseph. He really had no complaints. But this situation was not the perfect will of God for him. Sometimes we can get too comfortable where we are. God still is in control of our life and wants the perfect picture developed. Remember, God has a perfect timing for everything.

A second test of Joseph's faith came through Potiphar's wife. She tied to seduce Joseph, but Joseph, being a man of integrity and love for God, fled the scene. When he turned away to escape Potiphar's wife, she pulled off his coat. She used it as evidence and had Joseph put into prison. Everything went from good to bad in just a few minutes.

But again, God was with Joseph and showed him mercy and gave him favor in the eyes of the keeper of the prison. Joseph's gift of interpretation of dreams that God had put in him began to surface there in the jail. The chief butler of the king was in prison too. He had a dream and Joseph interpreted the dream. The butler was released from prison, just like Joseph had spoken, but he forgot about Joseph for two years.

Finally, the call came from Pharaoh himself. He had a dream and no one in the kingdom could interpret it. The butler's memory was jolted and he remembered Joseph, who was still in prison. Joseph was brought before Pharaoh and immediately gave the words of wisdom. Promotion came after he interpreted the Pharaoh's dream, and he became second in command of Egypt.

Joseph's father, Jacob, had long since accepted the fact that Joseph was dead. The coat of many colors had been shown to him covered with blood. But in actuality, it was animal blood, not Joseph's. This was false evidence appearing real. Jacob had allowed what he saw and heard to kill his hope for Joseph's future. Many years had passed, and Jacob lived these years with great sorrow.

During a great famine that was affecting the land, Jacob sent his sons to Egypt to seek assistance. He had heard there was food there. In Egypt, the brothers encountered Joseph, who was in command of the storehouses. There, the dream began to be fulfilled as they bowed before their brother (although at first they did not know it was he) whom they were sure they would never see again.

Joseph's brothers had to go back and confess to their father what they had done. When Jacob heard the news he cried, "My son Joseph is still alive!"

Just because you do not understand where you are today and cannot see the rhyme or reason for the way your life has gone, do not give up hope. God is with you in the bad times as well as the good times. He is there in the darkness as well as in the light. God has not left you, but is always present, developing you and preparing you for the time the "seed" bursts forth and become the fruitful tree.

It does not matter where you are and what has happened in your life. God is faithful not to forget His promise to you. His creative power is still working on your behalf. That "seed" of promise in your spirit will burst forth and produce the intention of its purpose. We have purpose in this life and God wants it to become reality.

The vision and Word from God was not dead. God is faithful.

Jesus is the Great Example

But Jesus answered them, saying "The hour has come that the son of Man be glorified. Most assuredly I say to you, unless a grain of wheat falls into the ground and dies, it remains alone; but if it dies, it produces much grain" (John 12:23-24).

Jesus was the "'seed" of the woman that God prophesied

would bruise the head of the serpent. "And I will put enmity between you and the woman, and between your seed and her Seed: he shall bruise your head, and you shall bruise His heel" (Gen. 3:15 NKJV).

Jesus was there when God said, "Let Us make man in Our image" (Gen. 1:26 NKJV). He knew who He was and the purpose of his becoming the "seed of the woman." Jesus knew He was the Redemptive Plan of God, purposed to redeem mankind and restore the human race back to position that God had intended for it in the beginning.

Even though He went about doing good things and healing the multitudes, Jesus knew the ultimate plan was His *death* and then His *resurrection*. Jesus had to have His garden of Gethsemane experience where He submitted totally to the will of His Father. He knew the hour had come for Him to become the supreme sacrifice. During those dark night hours, He was alone. The disciples could not stay awake to pray with Him. Jesus agonized in prayer until drops of blood began to drop from His forehead. He was beginning to feel the separation from His Father that was going to happen a few hours later. He agonized, yet He submitted to the perfect will of His Father.

He prophesied His death and resurrection to the disciples. He had to become the "seed" that would have to die and be put in the ground so that much grain (fruit) would be produced.

We also have to learn to let go and allow God to take control of our vision and dream. The "seed" is only going to respond to God's timing. God will create the environment for the seed to be nurtured and burst forth with all the fullness that it will produce.

From the looks of things, the "vision" and "dream" God the Father had for Jesus been destroyed. Darkness rushed in and it was only the middle of the day. Jesus gave up His spirit. It looked as though Satan had won. But on the third day, Jesus Christ came forth out of the tomb victorious over death, hell, and the grave. Now the fruit of that seed and the law of increase could become a reality. The church was born and 3,000 were added to the church when the first Gospel message was proclaimed by Peter. (See Acts 1).

"Yet it pleased the Lord to bruise Him, He has put Him to Grief. When you make His soul an offering for sin, He shall see His seed, He shall prolong His days, and the pleasure of the Lord shall prosper n His hand. He shall see the labor of his soul, and shall be satisfied." (Isa. 53:10-11 NKJV)

"For it became him, for whom are all things, and by whom are all things, in bringing many sons unto glory, to make the captain of their salvation perfect through sufferings." (Heb. 2:10 NKJV)

Don't Bury Your Dream or Vision

God wants you to have the best in your life. What is it that you desire? What dream seed and vision has God placed in the deep crevices of your spirit? He is waiting for you to verbalize your dream and vision.

You may be facing heartache today because your dreams have been shattered by unexpected circumstances. The enemy of your soul may be screaming in your ear, "It's all over. There is nothing you can do about it. It's dead. God has forsaken you." But my friend, I am here to encourage you to rise up in faith like the Shunammite woman did. Don't lose faith in the vision or dream. Remember, God planted the "dream seed" in the deep crevices of your spirit. Your Lord is the one who called you and He is the one who birthed the vision. God will not let the vision perish but will breathe new life into it so that it will be better than before.

Yogi Berra, the famous and colorful catcher for the New York Yankees and a member of the Baseball Hall of Fame is also famous for the following quote: "It ain't over till it's over." We all need to get that same attitude in our heart.

Do not bury your vision or dream. Don't let discouragement or fear sabotage your mind. Refuse to speak doubt and unbelief, even though it goes against everything that is happening. Be like the Shunammite woman and cry out, "All is well." Do not accept anything less than what God has promised you. Remember, God is Truth. Circumstances are not the truth. Hang in there and continually allow praise and the Word of God to pass through your lips. Let God bring your dream back to life with His resurrection power.

God does not expect us to do the impossible in our own strength.

CHAPTER FIVE

THE APPOINTED TIME FOR YOUR VISION

"God is always right on time! He will perfect that which concerns me and complete His works that He has begun."

CHAPTER 5

THE APPOINTED TIME FOR YOUR VISION

"But You, O LORD, shall endure forever, And the remembrance of Your name to all generations. You will arise and have mercy on Zion; For the time to favor her, Yes, the set time, has come."
– Psalm 102:12-13 NKJV

For those who might be unaware of what is going on around them, an appointed time is, in truth, an open display of the sovereignty and power of God. In this display, we discover with certainty that nothing is impossible with God. In this season—the appointed time—God fulfills His will, both for you and for His kingdom. In so doing, he also fulfills his promises and the dreams of his people.

There is an appointed time for everyone. There is an appointed time for Israel. There is an appointed time for you and me. If the Lord has promised it, He will certainly bring it to pass.

Recall again the Scriptures concerning Abraham and Sarah. They both had walked in faith for a quarter of a century anticipating the promise of God. Finally, as they neared one hundred years of age, the Lord told Abraham. "Is anything to hard for the Lord? At the appointed time, I will return to you, according to the time of life, and Sarah shall have a son" (Gen. 18:14 NKJV). One year later, "at the appointed time," Isaac was born to aged parents. "For Sarah conceived and bore Abraham a son in his old age, at the set time of which God had spoken to him" (Gen. 21:2 NKJV).

While there are, indeed, appointed times of judgment (Jesus speaks of the end time) but declares that "no man knows, not even the angels in heaven, nor the Son, but only the Father" (Mark 13:32 NKJV). The phrase most frequently represents a time, preset by God, when He reveals "wonders, plans formed long ago, [that unfold} with perfect faithfulness" (Isa. 25:1 NKJV).

Demons may stand arrayed against the Lord; nations may align themselves to fight Him. It does not matter! "The Lord laughs at him,
For He sees that his day is coming (Ps. 119:91 NKJV). Even God's enemies' plans for evil are reversed and made to serve His purposes.

God wants you to come to the place in your walk with the Lord where you have a clear understanding of the Scripture, "And we know that all things work together for good to those who love God, to those who are the called according to His purpose" (Rom. 8:28 KJV).

You may not understand why certain events are happening in your life. It may seem that all hope for the dream and vision that you had is destroyed. You may be walking aimlessly in life with no purpose. You have entered into a survival mode of living instead of walking in the favor and abundance of God. I am here to tell you not to give up. Do not throw your hope away. Whatever negative things have happened, just realize and know that God is aware of every event. He will reverse the curse against you. He will cause your eyes to be opened so you will know that He has led you to the place where you can rise with the favor of God in your life.

I know it seems that door to your dream will never open, but God has the door no man can shut or any demon withstand. I have a heart for those who have a special call and gifting in their life. I have been there and know the frustration of things not going as they should.

God will give you instructions. Maybe on your bed of slumber at night, or through a godly man or woman. God has the specific instructions that will lead you into triumph and the fulfillment of your dream and vision.

God brought a Scripture to light for me some time ago: "But may the Lord God of all grace, who called us to His eternal glory by Jesus Christ, after you have suffered for a while, perfect, establish, strengthen, and settle you" (1 Pet. 5:10 KJV). The word "perfect" is not the same translation of the Greek word *teleioo* that means, "to perfect" in the sense of "to make spiritually mature and complete." *Teleioo* means, "to fit or join together." The predominating idea in the verb is adjustment, the putting of parts into right relationship and connection with one another. Another way to describe this verb is "to fit like a piece of a puzzle fitting snugly in place."

Sometimes difficulties in our lives are sent to press you into the center of God's perfect will. God's purpose will always be the foremost thing in His eyes. He will never forsake you but will always be there in the middle of the trial. He was present in the middle of the "fiery furnace" when Shadrach, Meshach, and Abed-Nego were thrown into the fire to be destroyed. But God delivered them and they came out of the fire without even the smell of smoke on their garments. God sent an angel to shut the lions' mouths when Daniel was thrown in the midst of them. Promotion was given to each of these men when they all came out of the negative situation. God was glorified and His divine purpose was fulfilled for all of them. (See Daniel 3:8-30 and Daniel 6:10-23.)

God Gives Vision and Hope and Dreams

If God gave you a vision, a spiritual hope, or a dream for your future, there will be an appointed time when that which God spoke comes to pass. Thus, the Lord assures us: "Write the vision and make it plain on tablets, that he may run who reads it. For the vision is yet for an appointed time, but at the end it will speak and will not lie. Though it tarries, wait for it, because it will surely come. It will not tarry" (Hab. 2:2-3 NKJV).

If you have a vision or promise from God, that vision also has a time of fulfillment. Write it down and place it where you can see it every day. Though it tarries, wait for it. For it will certainly come to pass at the appointed time.

There is a miracle that was recorded in the 1940s. It is the Betty Baxter story. She had a muscular disease that caused her body to be twisted and deformed. She could not walk, feed herself, and clothe herself. Her feet were so deformed she could not even put on a shoe. Many had prayed for her, but it seemed as if nothing was happening.

God appeared to her in the night and told her that at 3:00 p.m. on Sunday, God's power would be manifested and she would receive a miracle healing. Betty told everyone about her vision. Most were skeptical and full of unbelief. Betty had her mother buy her a brand new pair of shoes for that day. She knew that the appointed time for her miracle (her dream) was near.

The crowd gathered at her home. Betty was brought outside on a bed because of the crowd. At 3:00 p.m., you could hear a pin drop. Suddenly, the air resounded with popping and cracking. Betty's deformed body untwisted in front of dozens of witnesses, transforming into the shape of a normal, healthy young woman. Betty stood, put on her new shoes, and began to dance and praise God.

Betty Baxter never went back into that prison of hopelessness. This was chronicled as one of the most miraculous miracles in modern church history. She shared her miraculous testimony for many years after the event in churches and revivals across America.

When the Lord manifests Himself openly in an appointed time, He actually moves through a power grid He established in a hidden place during the time of preparation. His work appears suddenly, but its preparation may have taken many years. Either way, an appointed time flows through appointed people. Your purpose and dream and vision will also burst forth in God's perfect timing.

He predestines the time of their breakthrough in advance, even as He works silently within their hearts in preparation.

Consider the Lord's word to His disciples: "You did not choose Me but I chose you, and appointed you that you would go and bear fruit, and that your fruit would remain" (John 15:16 NKJV). Every disciple feels that, at some point, he or she chose Christ. Yet, the deeper truth is that God chose us before the foundation of the world and has been working after He chose us. We could not even come to Christ had not the Father drawn us.

"Blessed be the God and Father of our Lord Jesus Christ, who has blessed us with every spiritual blessing in the heavenly places in Christ, Just as He chose us in Him before the foundation of the world, that we should be holy and without blame before Him in love, having predestined us to adoption as sons by Jesus Christ to Himself, according to the good pleasure of His will." (Eph. 1:3-5 NKJV)

"No one can come to Me unless the Father who sent me draws him; and I will raise him up at the last day." (John 6:44 NKJV)

Yet, He who chose us also appointed us to bear much fruit. The same power that worked surrender in us and then inspired our faith continues to work in our hearts throughout our days, appointing us to bear fruit. The idea that we can just sit quietly in church is a deception. You may look at your life and feel unfruitful. But God is not done with you yet.

Do you believe God has chosen you? Then believe also that He has appointed you to bear fruit. That "seed" that is inside your spirit has purpose. God's resurrection power is working right now, causing that seed to produce and manifest the power and purpose of God in your life.

GOD IS ALWAYS RIGHT ON TIME!
HE WILL PERFECT THAT WHICH CONCERNS ME AND COMPLETE HIS WORK THAT HE HAS BEGUN.

CHAPTER SIX

COPING WITH DISAPPOINTMENT

"Look at where you are and see your dreams as God sees the! You only had a portion of what God has planned, but now is the time to take a fresh look at what God is doing with your life."

CHAPTER 6

COPING WITH DISAPPOINTMENT

"He found him in a desert land, and in the howling waste of a wilderness; He encircled him, He cared for him, He guarded him as the pupil of His eye."
– Deuteronomy 32:10 NKJV

Have you ever blown it? Have you ever tried to force your dream to come to pass only to have it all fall apart? You feel like a total failure, humiliated, and embarrassed. You ask the questions, "Where did I go wrong? Why didn't I wait for the right timing?" Every person, one time or another in his or her life, experiences disappointment and failure. Life is not always the easiest thing to figure out. It is often difficult to navigate through the storms of life. The wind howls as we tread onward toward our destination. Sometimes it looks as if we will never reach the goal. Thoughts of throwing up our hands in total defeat crowd out any thoughts of victory.

No matter how much faith you have or how good a person you are, eventually something or somebody will shake your faith to its foundations. Usually the disappointments that disturb us the most are those caused by other people. This is the reason you need to let God's presence be real in your life. God's presence is what brings true joy and happiness. We cannot look to others to bring us joy. The psalmist David wrote: "in your presence is fullness of joy; and at your right hand are pleasures for evermore"

(Ps.16:11 NKJV).

Life can be complicated. You appear to be in the middle of nowhere on the way to nowhere, yet you must always remember that you have a guide. Can you imagine having a life dream about something, shifting your entire life around that dream coming to fruition, and suddenly seeing it all fall apart? Some of you can imagine it because you are at that kind of place in life right now. Yet, as hurtful as every letdown may be, God can still lead you to a good place.

Great losses have been in many of your lives. The loss of a loved one, a loss of a job, and relationships destroyed through misunderstandings. Losses make you feel empty on the inside. You feel unworthy and helpless due to the circumstances. You are sure that it will take a miracle to restore your faith. .

If we are honest, we will admit that we feel emotionally and mentally wounded when a door closes on something we expected would be a great opportunity. The pain of the wound exhausts us. If we stay at the point of exhaustion, we become disillusioned and everything that we see in life is viewed through the eyes of our pain. This process begins to disarm our hope about life, our future, and ultimately, about God.

Did you know that a *disappointment* is ultimately a *God appointment*? Many people want God to guide them, and they even pray that God would order their steps, which is a great prayer to pray: "Direct my steps by Your Word; and let no iniquity have dominion over me" (Ps. 119:133 NKJV).

In Deuteronomy 32, Moses spoke these words to the nation Israel. He related their history of being chosen and blessed. Then he spoke of the disappointment they became to their God through their greed and disobedience. But then, Moses gave them a message of hope to show them God's love and forgiveness. He finished with God's promise of atonement and restoration to His people.

Moses knew by experience the feeling of abandonment and being a total failure. Because of his own stubbornness and taking things in his own hands in Egypt, he ended up on the backside of a desert. He got ahead of God and was moved by his natural instincts to react to the situation rather than wait on God for specific instructions. After forty years at the University of Failures, he had a supernatural encounter with God on top of Mount Horeb, the mountain of God. He had a "burning bush" experience. It was here that God revealed Himself to Moses and renewed the vision that was the property of Moses. (See Exodus 3 and 4.)

Now I believe that Moses did not come to the mountain of God by accident, but that he was there on purpose that day. In fact, I believe he was looking for any sign of God that would let him know that he was not alone. Forty years is a long stretch of time. For forty years he lived in obscurity. He was nobody. Before that, he had the status of being a prince in Egypt. He had advanced up the ladder of success and was in command. On the mountain, he was alone with his thoughts, the ones always running through his mind of who he could have been.

Isolation is always part of the desert experience. In this desolate place, we begin to imagine that we will lose our gifts and our usefulness to God. We imagine that God has left us behind and forgotten us. We are sure time is running out and all the good opportunities to be fruitful and successful are passing us by—that we are doomed to the desert.

If the desert causes such despondency, why does God allow the desert experience in our lives? Because in the desert, we are humbled. We are tested, and the true condition of our heart is revealed to us. There is nothing like the desert to find the real you. Your strengths and weaknesses will be revealed. God does not allow the desert experience to destroy you. He uses it to refine you. If you are currently in the desert, understand that God has not changed your vision or dream, but He is in the process of changing *you* so that you can fulfill that vision and dream. Don't give way to the feelings of being abandoned. Those are all lies of the enemy. God does four things for us in the desert: He encircles us. He cares for us. He guards us as the pupil of His eye. He guides us. (See Deuteronomy 32:10.)

The day that Moses turned aside to investigate why the bush was burning but not being consumed, God reassured Moses that his best days were ahead of him. It was a day of divine appointment. Mark it down. Things do not just happen. There is a God- arranged plan for this world that we are in, which includes a specific plan for each one of us.

That day, God began to speak to Moses on a personal basis. He called Moses by name from out of the flames of the bush. And Moses replied, "I'm here." Then God cried out, "Take off your sandals, because the place you stand is holy ground." The Hebrew word translated "holy" means "separated." God was telling Moses to separate himself from his past.

Then God said, "I am the God of Abraham, the God of

Isaac, and the God of Jacob." These men had experienced failure and disappointments. Had it not been for God's grace, not one of them would have accomplished anything worth remembering.

In other words, God was telling Moses that this was a time for a *second chance*. Most great men have failed, but God never gave up on them. He takes ordinary men and allows them to do extraordinary things. God will never change His mind about you and the dream and vision that he birthed in your spirit. Do not be inhibited by your past failures. Yesterday is in the tomb, but tomorrow is still in the womb. Allow the presence of God to flood your being with His peace and joy. Do it today!

I want to point out three of the most common mistakes made by individuals who are called to do great things on this earth.

We Run Before We Are Sent

The first mistake is that we run before we are sent. This problem is caused by *intensity*. When I was at the young age of twenty-two, God put a call on my life to preach the Word of God. I had completed four years of Bible college in Houston, Texas. I was employed at the time with Ford Marketing Corporation in the automotive parts warehouse. I rose early in the morning to be at work at 6:00 a.m. I spent time with my family in the evenings until they retired to bed. I would then get my Bible and study and pray for about an hour. I remember crying out to God to open the doors for the ministry. I was ready to go and preach. One night to my surprise, the Lord spoke to my spirit. It sounded like an audible voice, although it was not, but it was loud in my spirit. God said," You are like the messenger that ran to David, and when he got there, he did not have anything to say. You say you are ready to go set the world on fire, but you do not have any match to strike." Ouch! That hurt! God was letting me know that if I went right then, I would fail.

I got the message. The next few years of my life were spent being mentored by one of the greatest preachers of our century. I would not trade those years for anything. No amount of money could buy the wisdom and nuggets of gold that I received because I waited on God. As a young man, Moses had not heeded God's timing. He ran ahead of it, thinking he was going to deliver his people from bondage through violence. That was not God's plan at all, and Moses spent forty years in the desert, preparing for the right time

We Retreat After We Have Failed

Having run before we are sent, we end up shipwrecked and broken. Then what do we do? We find a hole to crawl into. *Insecurity* sets in. We hide. We cannot stand the thought of failure. We have already seen that failure, as painful as it is, can become an outstanding instructor. Moses knew he was called to deliver God's chosen people, but he chose to depend on his natural abilities and wisdom as a prince of Egypt to accomplish the most important plan for his life.

When he "ran ahead" of God's plan, the only alternative he had was to flee for his life when he realized the terrible mistake he had made. He fled as far away as possible, to the backside of the desert. He took on the appearance as a shepherd, hoping no one would recognize him as the one who had been second in command in Egypt. Now he was Moses the sheep herder, doing what he could do to survive.

We Resist When We Are Called

When God finally does call us, we resist. This is brought about by *inferiority.* Moses was not merely being humble when he made excuses why he could not do what God called him to do. He was feeling inferior.

His first excuse was that he would not be recognized as a spiritual leader. After all, he had already failed in his attempt to show who he was and his importance. Excuse number two was spoken from his lips. “"But suppose they will not believe me or listen to my voice; suppose they say, 'The LORD has not appeared to you' " (Exod. 4:1). But God revealed His power unto Moses through the simple rod that was in his hand. God proved to Moses that day that whatever he had, God would use for His glory.

Even after the display of God's sovereign power Moses had yet another excuse. He said that he was not eloquent, but was slow of speech and slow of tongue. But once again, God spoke and confirmed to Moses that He would use his brother Aaron to be his spokesperson and speak the words that God would give to Moses. God does not leave any detail unaddressed. He always provides the solution to complete His perfect will.

You may be hearing God reissue the call to you. But you are feeling unworthy and useless at this time because of your past failure or your inferiority complex. God knows your natural weakness. He wants you to become dependent upon His wisdom and power. All men fall. The great ones simply get back up. Yesterday's failure can become today's success. Tragedies can become triumphs. No matter how many times you fail, remember that failure is never final. Failure opens doors to start again. Falling only hurts for a season. Starting over brings new life.

"The Lord upholds all that fall, and raises up all those that are bowed down." (Ps. 145: 14 NKJV)

Every person will have the opportunity to fail. King David knew what it meant to fail and be on the brink of losing it all. He wrote in the Psalms these enlightening Scriptures:

"Before I was afflicted I went astray, but now I keep your Word." (Ps. 119:67 NKJV)

"It is good for me that I was afflicted, that I may learn your statues. The law of your mouth is better to me than thousands of coins of gold and silver pieces." (Ps. 119: 71-72 NKJV)

The Living Bible says it like this: "I used to wander off until you punished me; now I closely follow all you say ... The punishment you gave me was the best thing that could have happened to me, for it taught me to pay attention to your laws. They are more valuable to me than millions in silver and gold." Here, King David is describing his dark and dismal experience with failure and the two things he learned about failure:

Experiencing Failure Promotes An Obedient Life. When I go through times of failure, I am more than ever prompted to live in obedience. Someone notably said, "Actually it isn't the fall that hurts … but it's that sudden stop at the bottom!"

Experiencing Failure Prompts A Teachable Spirit. After failure, you come to God and His Word in desperation to learn from God and renew your fellowship with Him. Timing is as important as action. How many times have we done the right thing at the wrong time? God not only plans what we are to do, He has also arranged the right time for us to do it. Here is some godly advice: When God is in it, it flows. When the flesh is in it, it's forced. Let's not focus on our loss; focus on what is left. God will make our future bright.

Failure doesn't mean you are a failure … it does mean you have not succeeded yet.

Failure doesn't mean you have accomplished nothing … it does mean you have learned something.

Failure doesn't mean you have been a fool … it does mean you had a lot of faith.

Failure doesn't mean you have been disgraced … it does mean you were willing to try.

Failure does not mean you are inferior … it does mean you are not perfect.

Failure doesn't mean you have wasted your life … it

does mean you have a reason to start afresh.

Failure doesn't mean you should give up ... it does mean you must try harder.

Failure doesn't mean you will never make it ... it doe mean it will take a little longer.

Failure doesn't mean that God has abandoned you ... it does mean God has a better idea.

Failure is usually followed by deep disappointment. Disappointment is not just a sad state of mind. Deep disappointment actually can sever our hearts from our faith. Disappointment is the enemy's work. Demonically manipulated disappointment can actually "dis-appoint a person from God's destiny for his life. Even "good Christians" are vulnerable. In many cases you will find that, at some point, a believer who has fallen away fell into deep disappointment about some failed *spiritual expectation.*

I have known many who were doing well, moving toward their appointed destiny. The future God had for them seemed close enough to taste. Then they became disappointed in someone or something. By accepting into their souls this demonically manipulated disappointment, their faith turned dormant; a bitter winter took over their souls. It is there, even in the throes of disappointment, that the righteous learn to live by faith.

Brokenness can leave people without faith for the future. People lose loved ones through death. Others have had their spouse leave them for someone else. Don't let your fracturing experiences shape your future. Never believe in your hurts. Believe in your dreams. Consider this quote by

Sir Winston Churchill: "If we open a quarrel between past and present, we shall find that we have lost the future."

Habakkuk, the prophet, had this to tell us. "Write the vision, and make it plain upon tablets, that he may run that reads it. For the vision is yet for an appointed time, but at the end it shall speak, and not lie: though it tarry, wait for it; because it will surely come, it will not tarry" (Hab. 2:1-4 NKJV).

We all face times of disappointment. I went through a time when the promise of God seemed like a foolish spiritual fantasy. For nearly five years, I had not been involved in pastoral ministry. No doors would open. God was doing a work in my soul to cause me to trust Him, but I felt abandoned and cut off from my calling. In a moment of abject honesty, I prayed, "Lord, You promised that those who believed in You would not be disappointed. Master, You know all things. Look at my heart. I am full of disappointment." The Lord simply replied, "Your life is not over." Of course, I knew that. I was a healthy man. Yet the spell of disappointment had flooded my soul with darkness, causing me to conclude erroneously that God was done with me.

Listen well, my friend. Satan can stop our destiny if we accept the power of disappointment into our lives. Once we accept the heaviness of a deep disappointment, backsliding is often close behind. You see, dis-appointment cuts us off from our vision, and without a vision, people perish.

"Where there is no revelation, people cast off restraint; but blessed is the one who heeds wisdom's instructions."

(Prov. 29:18 NIV)

See your dream through the eyes of God. See your dream through eyes of faith. Learn to wait upon God. During this time of waiting, your strength will be renewed, and you will be strong.

"But they that wait upon the Lord shall renew their strength; they shall mount up with wings as eagles; they shall run, and not be weary; and they shall walk and not faint." (Isa. 41:31 KJV)

God is completing the vision and dream that He designed for you before you were born. Many people wander in life with opinions, but you can be different because you have found direction for your life. Stop and let God define your vision. Look at where you are and see your dreams as God sees them. You only had a portion of what God has planned, but now is the time to take a fresh look at what God is doing with your life.

"For I know the thoughts that I think towards you, thoughts of peace and not evil, to give you a future and hope." (Jer. 29:11 NKJV)

HE WILL PERFECT THAT WHICH CONCERNS ME AND COMPLETE HIS WORK THAT HE HAS BEGUN.

CHAPTER SEVEN

YOU CAN PROPHESY YOUR FUTURE

"Faith's Confession is predicting the future conditions of things. To prophesy is to foretell something that is going to happen, before it actually happens. You can only prophesy what you can see (perceive) by faith."

CHAPTER 7

YOU CAN PROPHESY YOUR FUTURE

"Then Jesus turned to the captain and said, 'Go. What you believed could happen has happened.'"
– Matthew 8:13 MSG

The fulfillment of the vision and dream that God has placed inside your spirit is up to you. You are the deciding factor whether God's word in you will come to pass. You cannot place the blame on anyone for your failure. No other person controls your life. No one has the power to control your mind or your actions without your permission. People can *hinder* the success and dream, but they cannot stop God's plan and purpose.

The definition of the word "hinder" means, "to place an obstacle sharply in the path, metaphorically giving the meaning of detaining a person unnecessarily." (See Acts 24:4.) There is also the meaning of "putting hindrances in the way of reaching others, or returning to them." (See Romans 15:22 and 1 Thessalonians 2:18.) Paul, the apostle, was saying that Satan hindered him from coming to the churches. I want to note here that *hindrances do not stop the plan of God, but only delay it.*

We, as children of God, have to recognize the scheme of the enemy. Once the enemy's scheme is exposed, we have the authority to bind the powers of Satan and loose God's power to bring the desired results. All power belongs to God, and He has passed that authority to use the name of Jesus and speak victory. "And I will give you the keys of the kingdom of heaven, and whatever you bind on earth will be bound in heaven, and whatever you loose on earth will be loosed in heaven" (Matt. 16:19 NKJV).

Disappointed believers often say: "God promised it, but why doesn't He fulfill what He has said?" Or, "I received a number of prophecies from men of God. Why isn't anything happening?"

God uses men and women of God to speak into our lives. Many of these prophetic words usually confirm what God has already spoken to you. There are also times that God will speak a fresh word concerning your future through a prophet. But remember, God mapped out your future before you were ever born. Therefore, no prophetic word is really a new word or a new vision, because God already had placed that seed in your spirit. God will use godly men and women to speak to you concerning what is already programmed in your spirit. Many times a person is not aware of the gift or calling that is there until it is uncovered by the Spirit and revealed.

God is willing to work on our behalf, but we have to allow Him to do his will and fulfill the purpose that He has planned for us. God will work if we will let Him. Remember, the purpose and plan for your life is already programmed. Every promise of God is conditional. What we do and how we respond to God determines whether the vision and dream comes to fruition.

There are five points that I want to share with you concerning your dreams and vision being fulfilled:

1. *Choose Your Direction.* Many people are floundering in life with no definite direction from God. They are like a little boat without a compass or a rudder, just floating all over the sea of life with no defined purpose.

You can choose the direction of your destiny. You have the right to decide to follow God and His plan. God created you as a free moral agent to make your own choices. He did not create you as a robot. Some people, however, never see the master plan that God designed specifically for them. Because they never see the plan, these individuals never step out in faith to do extraordinary things. They lack ambition. They can only follow the demands and example of others.

In order for your God-designed purpose to succeed, all of your decisions have to be in harmony with the Word of God. You have heard people who say: "Well, the Lord told me to do this and the Lord told me to do that," even when their behaviors are in conflict with Scripture. Many times people set their own course and direct their life with sensual desires instead of that "perfect will of God."

I want you to decide right now that you are making a quality choice to please God and to fulfill that dream and vision that He planted inside your spirit.

2. *Sees As God Sees.* Hope is having that confident expectation in the promises of God. "Now faith is the substance of things hoped for and the evidence of things not seen" (Heb. 11:1 NKJV). "Now faith is the assurance (the

confirmation, the title deed) of things <we> hope for, being the proof of things <we> do not see and the conviction of their reality--faith perceiving as real fact what is not revealed to the senses" (AMP).

We determine our destiny and the vision being fulfilled in our life. Either you are letting things happen or you are making things happen. Hope causes us to begin to speak words concerning the dream and vision that is within us. Faith causes us to speak boldly concerning the vision. Your vision is your future. What you see through eyes of faith is your future. Remember the definition of the word "vision" is the ability to see something not actually visible yet.

3. *Speak Prophetically To Your Vision By Faith.* Jesus taught the disciples a lesson on faith and speaking to the tree. "And the Lord said, if you had faith as a grain of mustard seed, you would say unto this sycamine tree, be rooted up, and be planted in the sea; and it would obey you" (Luke 17:6 NKJV).

There is that word "seed" again. A seed has the capability of knowing what its future is. Every seed is pre-programmed in its genetic code. It comes with a set of instructions for its future. When sown in good quality soil, and given the proper water, oxygen, heat, and light, it will grow up into a mature plant that can perfectly reproduce itself, because of its programming.

Faith's confession is predicting the future conditions of things. To prophesy is to foretell something that is going to happen, before it actually happens. You can only prophesy what you can see (perceive) by faith. .

God demonstrated this principle of faith when He created the heavens and the earth. God *said*, "Let there be light." He used His words. Every tree, plant, star, planet, animal, and sea creature was a product of His words. He *spoke* the universe into existence. Because we are created in His image, we have the ability of God in us along with His Word, hidden in our hearts, ready to be spoken and bring our dreams and vision to pass.

In the Book of Ezekiel, we read the story of the prophet speaking life to a graveyard of dry, dead bones. Ezekiel was carried by God and set down in a valley full of dry bones. These bones represented a mighty army that at one time was victorious and had won many battles. But now, this great army was reduced to mere bones. The flesh had rotted off and all that was left were the skeletons. Probably through the years, the wild animals had ripped the skin and muscle sinew away and even tore the skeletons apart to where there were limbs missing. The heat of the sun had dried and bleached them. Not a breath of life remained.

The Lord asked Ezekiel the question, "Can these bones live again?" Ezekiel replied, "Lord, only you know."

Then the Lord told him, "Prophesy upon these bones, and say unto them. O you dry bones, hear the Word of the Lord." So Ezekiel prophesied as he was commanded and there was a noise, and behold a shaking, and the bones came together, bone to his bone. And then the sinews and the flesh came upon them, and the skin covered them above; but there was no breath in them. Then the Lord said, "Prophesy to the wind and say to the wind, thus says the Lord, come from the four winds, O breath, and breathe upon those slain, that they might live. prophesy to the four winds, O breath, and breathe upon these slain, that they may live." So he prophesied as he was commanded, and the breath came into them, and they lived, and stood upon their feet, an exceeding great army. (Ezek. 37:1-14 KJV)

This once-successful army of warriors was now resurrected with new life and vision. Each limb that had been severed went right to the place it belonged. Nothing was lacking or missing. Some of you have started with your vision and dream, but came to a place where it was destroyed. Everything is now, or seems to be, hopeless, dead on the inside. But I am here to tell you there is a prophetic word being spoken to you today. God is saying to you: there is hope. You will rise again with new strength and life. You will be equipped with everything that you need to accomplish the dream. When God moves, no foe can resist or stand in His presence. God is not through with you yet. He will perfect that which concerns you and complete His work that He has begun.

4. *Water The Seed With The Word.* Every seed that is planted in the ground requires water to allow it to grow and produce. Many dream seeds have not been cared for in the garden of our spirit. The seed needs food to survive. It needs moisture to help germinate and begin to sprout into the plant it was programmed to be.

The sad thing is, many dreams and visions are lying

dormant in the dry ground, because food and moisture were withheld. Many people live their lives on this earth without fulfilling that dream that God put in them. There are spiritual laws that have to be obeyed in order for it all to come to pass. It does not just happen. Every promise is conditional. The Lord said many times throughout the Scriptures that if we will obey his commands, He would perform His word.

Salvation was paid for at the cross, burial, and resurrection of Jesus Christ the Son of God. Paul wrote in Romans 10:8-10: "But what says it? The word is nigh you, in your mouth, and in your heart: that is, the word of faith, which we preach: because if you shall confess with your mouth Jesus as Lord, and shall believe in your heart that God raised him from the dead, you shall be saved: for with the heart man believes unto righteousness; and with the mouth confession is made unto salvation" (NKJV). You have to speak the word declaring Jesus is Lord and that God raised Him from the dead. Then you are saved. This is a spiritual law that has to be activated in order for it to become a reality in your life. Satan cannot stop the new birth of an individual when this law of faith is obeyed.

Now we need to find Scriptures in the Word of God that pertain to you and your particular vision. Begin to water that dream seed daily with the Word of God. The Bible says in Isaiah 55:10-11, "For as the rain comes down, and the snow from heaven, and does not return there, but waters the earth, and make it bring forth and bud, that it may give seed to the sower and bread to the eater. So shall my Word be that goes forth from my mouth. It shall not return to Me void, but it shall accomplish what I please, and it shall prosper in the thing for which I sent it" (NKJV).

What you see and what you think dictates your level of truth. If you can't believe that your dream can come to pass, forget it for now; you are not pregnant with it yet. You have to recognize that those godly desires inside you are seeds ready to be birthed. The Bible says in Hebrews 11:3, "By faith we understand that the worlds were framed by the Word of God, so that the things which are seen were not made of things that were visible" (NKJV).

You must believe it! Jesus said that if you can believe, that mountain in the way of your seeing your dream come to pass can be removed.

"According to your faith, be it unto you." (Matt. 9:29 NKJV)

"Go your way; and as you have believed, so let it be done for you." (Matt. 8:13 NKJV)

"Therefore I say to you, whatever things you ask when you pray, believe that you receive them, and you will have them." (Mark 11:24 NKJV)

What you see regulates your life. The way you see and perceive things is vitally important. The eye is the light of the body. How you see and perceive things determines how you act or react to the conditions and opportunities of life around you. Believe that you will succeed in bringing the reality of your vision and dream into the reality of the natural realm.

"The lamp of the body is the eye: if therefore your eye is single, your whole body shall be full of light. But if your eye is evil, your whole body shall be full of darkness. If therefore the light that is in you be darkness, how great is the darkness!" (Matt. 6:22-23 NKJV)

Abraham walked in faith not considering his own body, which was dead reproductively speaking, since he was almost 100 years old, and the deadness of Sarah's womb. He simply spoke the Word of God and His promises to Abraham. He called those things that did not exist as though they did. In other words he "saw and perceived" as God did. (See Romans 4:13-31.)

5. Develop Patience and Allow God To Work. We have discovered that faith is the spiritual force that brings substance. Patience is the "power twin" of faith. These two are co-workers together in our lives. The power of patience is a working power. When your faith has a tendency to waiver, it is patience that comes to faith's aid to help make it stand. Almost everywhere you find faith mentioned in the Bible, you also find patience.

Traditionally, we think of patience as knuckling under and being satisfied with whatever comes our way. But that is not what patience is. Patience is a real force that has to be developed. It literally means being constant or being the same all the time. It is steadfast despite opposition, difficulty, or adversity. Patience guards against admitting a doubt or having a confession of fear.

NOTHING IS IMPOSSIBLE TO HIM WHO BELIEVES

CHAPTER EIGHT

YOUR VISION DOMINATES YOUR LIFE

"So today, I want to encourage you to focus on your vision and dream. Let it dominate your thinking and let your actions reveal your faith in what God has promised."

CHAPTER 8

YOUR VISION DOMINATES YOUR LIFE

"Blessed is the man whose delight is in the law of the Lord."

– Psalm 1:1-2 NKJV

God created you with a passion to excel with your vision. The moment the blueprint for your dream and vision is unfolded before you is when you will realize this is not just a dream, but it is real. From that moment on, every thought is focused on finishing the course with much joy. Every decision that you make will affect your future.

When God makes His plan clear for your life, perhaps nudging you in a brand new direction, it is important that you be very sensitive how you communicate this to others. You cannot assume that everybody knows all that you know about this process God has for you. Others may not greet the idea with immediate acceptance and open arms. Communicate your thoughts with tenderness, care, and concern. Pushing and rushing into a plan without concern, understanding, and blessing can create relational roadblocks that may shadow and hamper the effectiveness of future ministry.

When it is time for the vision to move forward, the *plan will flow.* When you are in the center of God's will, my friend, it *flows*. It does not have to be forced. The Scriptures declare, "When a man's ways please the Lord, he makes even his enemies to be at peace with him" (Prov. 16:7 NKJV).

Are you having major problems and strife with those who are close to you? It may be time to step back and ask why. Begin on your knees by asking, "Father, are my ways pleasing to You? Is there something I am missing or overlooking here?" Be open and sensitive in your heart. These self-examination sessions before the Lord, painful as they might be, will yield benefit and fruit for years to come.

It is a fresh assurance to be moving in the direct current of God's will. Perhaps this is where you are right now. You know that you are in the center of God's will. It is a humbling place to live but the best place in the whole world.

It will take a genuine faith to step out and begin to do the things that God has mapped out for you in the blueprint for your vision. Have you made that move, following the nudging of God, into realms you would not have dreamed of five years ago?

Faith is indeed the greatest miracle-working power imaginable. Faith never fails a person; you fail when you give up on your faith.

Remember, faith is like a seed. If a seed is not planted, it cannot bear fruit. But planting is just the first phase. Unless the seed is watered, it will not sprout. Once the seed is planted and watered, growth will begin. But unless the plant is nourished, it will not reach full maturity and will not blossom.

When buds are beginning to form, if the proper climatic conditions do not exist, the stalk will produce no fruit. Bearing fruit is the final stage of the seed's producing. This is the same with our vision and dream. Faith begins when you begin to believe in the ideas that God gives you. Then you must ask yourself, "Will my faith, acted upon and firmly embraced, cause my life and my activity to be an inspiration to somebody to become a better person or to achieve more in his or her life, to further God's kingdom?"

It a certainty that the enemy of your soul will bring hindrances against the vision and dream that God has birthed in you. There will always be obstacles that stand in the way of your progress. Remember, hindrances do not stop God's plan, they only bring a temporary delay. When you are faced with a mountain standing in your way, do not quit. Keep on striving until you climb over, find a passage through, tunnel underneath, or simply stay and turn the mountain into a gold mine and dig out all the gold that you can.

Do not allow the mountain to detour you away from the path of blessing that God has you on. *What you believe regulates your life.* Jesus said, "For assuredly, I say to you, whoever says to this mountain, 'Be removed and be cast into the sea,' and does not doubt in his heart, but believes that those things he says will be done, he will have whatever he says" (Mark 11:23 NKJV). Whatever you have been saying is what will follow you, whether it is bad or good.

If you have been saying, "Woe is me, everything is bad," then that is what will follow you. On the other hand, if you have been saying, "I am blessed. I am more than a conqueror. I can do all things through Christ who is my strength. God prospers me so I can fulfill my dream and vision," these things will follow you.

Jesus gave a faith lesson in Mark 11:24. He says:

"Therefore I say to you, whatever things you ask when you pray, believe that you receive them, and you will have them" (NKJV). You say what you believe. What you believe is what you think. And what you think is actually what you see or perceive. You have to believe that the dream and vision will come to pass.

There are several points I want to make concerning your vision dominating your life.

1. **Don't look back.** Looking backward stops progress. Many people spend their lives looking in the rearview mirror thinking about what could have been, what should have been, always dwelling on the pains of yesterday. God wants to give us beauty for our ashes, joy for our mourning, rejoicing for our heaviness. The key is you have to let go of the ashes before God can give you the beauty.

2. **Looking at difficulties depresses.** Sometimes the situation that you are facing can overwhelm you. The enemy will magnify the problem and cause you to see yourself as a loser. The weight of the problem causes you not to see the desired results of your vision and dream. Suddenly you feel as if you are all alone and that nobody really cares. Loneliness breeds disappointment and despair and then eventually despondency and depression invade your mind. If you allow these thoughts to dominate your thinking then there is no alternative but defeat.

The word "possibility" should always be in our thoughts

and conversation. Remember that God is the one who causes the "impossible" to become "possible." Jesus taught His disciples this principle. He said, "With men it is impossible, but not with God; for with God all things are possible" (Mark 10:27 NKJV).

If you will put your life in God's hands, He will remove the obstacles from your pathway and bring you to your appointed goal. You have the "spirit of a champion;" you are the one who finishes the race. You were born to win. God is with you and there is nothing that you can't do.

3. **Do not allow fear to dominate you**. Someone described fear as **False Evidence Appearing Real.** However, "God has not given us a spirit of fear (timidity) but of power and love and of a sound mind" (2 Tim. 1:7 NKJV). This means when you surrender to fears, you can be sure the fears did not come from God. The largest fear we face is the fear of failure. There is no need to fear "because I can do all things through Christ who strengthens me" (Phil.4:13 NKJV). You can become the person that God has intended for you to be and all His promises will be fulfilled.

4. **Do not let your past or your fear of the future destroy your happiness today.** Happiness is a Now Place. Someone stated this truth: "Yesterday is in the tomb; tomorrow is in the womb, your life is today." TODAY IS THE ONLY PLACE YOU WILL EVER EXIST. When you get to your future, you will rename it "Today." The psalmist declared: "This is the day that the Lord hath made; we will rejoice and

be glad in it" (Ps. 118:24 NKJV). Winston Churchill made this statement: "If we open a quarrel between past and present, we shall find that we have lost the future."

5. **Do not allow fences to influence your dreams and vision**. Many people have allowed themselves to be fenced in and contained. The vision that was birthed in their hearts has not progressed. Fences are limiting concepts that you allow to influence your goals and dreams. These fences are negative self-image perceptions such as (1) I don't know the right people; (2) I don't have an education; (3) I don't have enough money.

You can determine your destiny when you focus on your vision and dream. Your focus will determine the direction your life takes. You will either let things happen or you will make things happen. The choice is yours.

6. **You must ask what you want or take what you get.** Once you get a momentum of success going, it will generate more success. Success breeds success. The anointing that you respect is the anointing that increases in your life. Focus on your vision and purposely be in the presence of those of like vision. Allow the wisdom and anointing to be imparted to you for your success. God has allowed me to have great men of God as my mentors in life. By observing their life and allowing them to impart into my life, I have witnessed good results for the vision and dream that God birthed in me.

Your vision is your future. Begin to focus on the vision

and be diligent to do whatever God requires to see it fulfilled. If you do not have a vision or a dream, then you simply do not have a meaningful and purposeful future. Many people never realize their full potential in life because they never see by the things that are not seen. Why is this true? Because "things which are seen were not by things which do appear" (Heb. 11:3 NKJV). Where there is no vision, there is no future, because your vision is your future. A vision is the ability to see something not actually visible.

So today, I want to encourage you to focus on your vision and dream. Let it dominate your thinking and let your actions reveal your faith in what God has promised.

Romans 1:5 talks about "obedience by faith." I love the two words and the way they work together.

If I have faith, I *believe* He has a *plan*.

If I have sincere faith, I *believe* He has a *better plan*.

If I have obedient faith, *I believe* He has *the plan.*

Faith tells me I am His. Faith tells me He's my <u>Dad</u> ... my <u>Savior</u> ... my <u>Future</u> ... my <u>Hope</u>.

There will never be another now so I will make the most of today.

There will never be another me so I will make the most of myself.

CHAPTER NINE

DEALING WITH ADVERSITY TO YOUR VISION

"Choose today to hold on to God's Promises. God knows what challenges you face, and He has a way to turn things around for your good. 'Let us hold fast the confession of our hope without wavering, for He who promised is Faithful'" (Heb. 10.23 NKJV)

CHAPTER 9

DEALING WITH ADVERSITY TO YOUR VISION

"Greater is He that is in you than he that is in the world."
– 1 John 4:4 KJV

It is inevitable. Adversity will stick up its ugly head, right in the middle of your fulfilling your vision. The enemy has one agenda: to stop God's plan from being fulfilled. Satan knows that you are a threat to him and his work to destroy the God's redemption plan for humankind. He despises you as much as he does Jesus, because you are a duplicate of Christ and have the ability to do what God has assigned you to do.

It is very important not to become perplexed at the first sign of adversity. Your attitude will make you or break you. Attitude is a position that you take as a result of your reaction to a situation. The greatest influence on whether we are happy or miserable depends on our dispositions, not on our circumstances. Let us have a positive attitude of "I can do all things through Christ who strengthens me" (Phil. 4:13 NKJV). A speaker at a conference once said: "Life is 10 percent of what happens to us and 90 percent how we respond to it."

There will always be circumstances that you did not anticipate. Either you will *react* to the problem or you will *act* in faith. Our reactions are spontaneous events—like being startled when someone jumps from behind a doorway and shouts "Boo!" The first reaction is fear. Something out of the dark or the unknown causes you to have sudden thoughts of being overwhelmed. Peter had this happen to him one night on a stormy sea. The storm was raging and tossing large destructive waves of water that could have destroyed all that was in the boat. But Jesus came walking on the water, defying the storm. Peter saw Him and desired to get out of the boat and walk to Him. Jesus responded, "Come." Without any hesitation, Peter stepped over the rail and began to walk on top of the waves just like Jesus. But then he took his eyes off Jesus, saw the tumultuous waves instead, became afraid and began to sink. But immediately, he called on the Lord Jesus who reached out his hand and lifted Peter above the waves and they walked back to the boat. The way we react or act determines our victory.

"Fear not. Stand still, and see the salvation of the Lord, which He will work for you today. The enemy you see today, you shall never see again." (Exod. 14:13 NKJV)

This Scripture declares that fear is not an option, but faith and resting in God's promises is the answer. Every problem has a limited life span. No problem is permanent. Every mountain has a peak. Every valley has its low point. Life has its ups and downs, its peaks, and its valleys. Problems do end. Storms always give way to the sun. Winter always thaws into springtime. **YOUR STORM WILL PASS!** Your problem will be resolved. When wisdom fails, when strength is no more, when the enemy seems to have you in his sights, know that God is on him and you will prevail.

Consider these three profound truths regarding your circumstances:

Circumstances that turn against us force dependence. When you find yourself in a situation that suddenly reverses field and goes in a direction you did not want it to go, you are humbled. This forces us into a position of dependence upon the Lord. This is exactly where God wants you. His wise approach is to keep you within the circle of His *protection* and *provision.* It is usually in these adverse circumstances that we find out what is really inside our spirits.

Circumstances that force dependence teach us patience. Oh, that dreaded word "patience." But how we need it. Most of us pray for patience and want it yesterday. When we are in this dependent position, we learn to wait on the Lord's perfect timing. We *learn* patience by practicing it. It is not produced in our life by just thinking, "I will be patient." It is produced when we make a quality decision to stand on the Word of God and go forward in life, not allowing the circumstances to make us adaptable to defeat. "And we also glory in tribulations (testing), knowing that tribulation (testing) produces perseverance (patience)" (Rom. 5:3 NKJV).

Circumstances that teach us patience make us wise. Wisdom becomes the gold crown of our adverse circumstances. The wisdom we glean from our experiences and from our testing of the Lord's promise will stay with us and bless us the rest of our lives. Maturity is evident in our lives as we walk in the wisdom that we have learned. When we attain wisdom, the circumstances we face today will not have the opportunity to reappear in the future. Why? Because through wisdom we have gained the ability to recognize the problem and solve it. Solomon said in the Book of Proverbs that "Wisdom is the principle thing, therefore get wisdom: and with all your getting get understanding" (Prov. 4:7 NKJV).

Circumstances should never be the regulator of our peace and joy. Circumstances are only temporary. They are always subject to change. Speaking the "Word" to them changes them. Learn to be thankful and to praise God in the circumstances. We do not thank God for the problem, sickness, or lack; but we are to have a thankful spirit in the midst of the circumstance. We are to thank God that He is Jehovah, that He is more than enough for whatever we are facing, and that He will bring us through to victory. "Thank God in everything—no matter what the circumstances may be, be thankful and give thanks. For this is the will of God for you who are in Christ Jesus" (1Thess.5:18 AMP). In actuality, God is changing you and your attitude and, in turn, the circumstances seem to change for your good.

In our quest to fulfill the vision and dream that God has given us, we will go through different seasons, or phases. Sometimes we may not understand all that happens. But, my friend, rest assured, God has one thing on His mind and that is for you to complete the race that is before you. There may be severe losses along the way, but God anticipated each day of your life. Sometimes a loss of a spouse or a relationship can knock you off course. But remember, God has your life mapped out. You are not the one to decide when someone has completed what God give you to do.

I am reminded of the Scripture where Paul wrote, "One plants, one waters, but God gives the increase" (1 Cor. 3:6 NKJV). God will allow one person to do his or her assignment and then allow the assignment to be completed and fulfilled by another. But remember that God brings the finished result. All we are required to do is be obedient and complete our assignment. There are different seasons in our lives. We have to adapt to God's Divine plan and allow Him to work all things for our good. Circumstances in our lives are only temporary. Do not let them get set in concrete. Perhaps you are coming in to a new season. Recognize it and allow this to be a season of fulfillment.

"To everything there is a season, a time for every purpose under heaven." (Eccles. 3:1 NKJV)

In my journey of faith with God, I learned three strong and life-sustaining truths from the book of Exodus. Through these truths, I learned that I do not walk alone, but God's presence is always evident.

1. ***Hard Times Do Not Erase God's Promises.*** When times seem difficult it is easy to leap to the conclusion that

God has forsaken us and forgotten His promises. In the book of Exodus, we can see God's care for Israel. They were enslaved in Egypt and were treated harshly by their captors. But God was still there with them. In this story we learn that when God says, "I promise," He never forgets it. We may forget. The whole nation may forget. But God cannot forget! And will not forget!

2. ***Harsh Treatment does not escape God's notice.*** God told Moses when he was receiving his instructions to deliver Israel, "I have indeed seen the misery of my people in Egypt. I have heard them crying out because of their slave drivers, and I am concerned about their sufferings. So I have come down to rescue them from the hand of the Egyptians" (Exod. 3:7-8 NIV). God is always aware! He cares very deeply! He will do whatever it takes to rescue His people. He will not abandon His own. God has a plan for the deliverance of all His children and will execute that plan at the right time.

3. ***Heavy tests do not eclipse God's concern.*** Regardless of the severity of the test you may be facing, it can never overshadow His concern. The nation Israel had been in captivity to the Egyptians for 400 years. Ten generations of people had suffered hard labor and harsh treatment from their captors. Their food had been limited and the people of God had been beaten severely, both physically and spiritually. Their morale was gone. They believed God had forsaken them and left them to be destroyed.

Perhaps this has been difficult times for you. The future

stretching out before you may seem gloomy or threatening. You may be crying out "Where is God?" He is right there with you. He has never left. Hudson Taylor, the great missionary to China, wrote on one occasion, "It doesn't matter how great the pressure is; what really matters is where the pressure lies. Whether it comes between you and God or presses you nearer to His heart."

You are not here by accident. God is looking for a man or woman, who will yield to His purposes and seize the day for His glory!

In order to walk through times of adversity and bear the fruit of your vision and dream, begin today to operate in the following biblical principles:

1. *Do not allow fear to paralyze you*. Allow me to reiterate something I said previously. *Fear is false evidence appearing real.* Fear is what destroys people's confidence in God and prevents them from moving forward in life and fulfilling the vision or dream that has been birthed in them. Fear is the devil's faith. Throughout the Bible, the Lord speaks through the prophets and apostles to the body of Christ to "fear not." When you surrender to fears, you can be sure the fears did not come from God.

2. *Have total trust in God.* Trust is a passive verb. It implies that you know God is in total control and you can "rest" with assurance that the Lord will not let you down.

When my daughter was a toddler. I put her on the table

and had her jump in my arms. At first, she was reluctant to do it, but after the first jump, she wanted to do it over and over again. I got tired and sat down. I did not realize she had crawled back up on the table. She yelled "daddy" and proceeded to jump. I frantically scrambled over to the table and caught her in the air just in time. She had total trust in her daddy to be there and knew that I would not let her get hurt. This is what God wants out of us today. He is saying, Trust Me! I will not fail you!

"Trust in the Lord with all your heart and lean not on your own understanding; in all your ways acknowledge Him, and He will make your paths straight." (Prov. 3:5-6 NKJV)

If you will put your life in God's hands, He will remove the obstacles from your pathway and bring you to your appointed goal. God's will can be accomplished in the life of a person only to the extent that he or she is willing to trust Him. Trust allows no lack of faith or confidence in God, no exceptions to God's plan and promises, no "ifs" in your prayers.

3. *Speak the Word of God concerning your vision.* What you say, either aloud or in your self-talk, in your time of adversity will have a great influence on how long you stay in that situation. In the book of James, the writer compares the tongue to the rudder of a large ship. Although the rudder is very small in comparison to the size of the ship, it controls the direction of the entire ship. This is a metaphor to show how your tongue will control the direction of your life. If

you are looking at the adverse storm or situation and speaking words of fear and failure, you will end up a defeated and discouraged individual because you are creating the atmosphere for defeat. Words make us or break us. In contrast, if you speak words of faith and victory, your spirit man will rise up and take charge. "Death and life are in the power of the tongue" (Prov. 18:21 NKJV). So, instead of talking about the adverse circumstances and how big that mountain is, speak God's promises concerning your vision and declaring how big *God* is. Create an environment of victory around you by speaking the Word of God boldly. The writer of Hebrews said that "By faith, we see the world was called into existence by God's word, by what we see created by what we don't see" (The Message). Your world (environment) is created by your words. Words of victory and confidence will create an environment of faith and hope. Others will be blessed by what they feel surrounding you.

You can maintain your dream and vision by confessing what God has declared in His Word. Keep the vision and dream before your eyes. Don't turn to the left or to the right, but keep looking forward and continually speak the dream and vision. We operate in the Kingdom of God and there is no room for demonic influence here. As long as you stay in His presence, acknowledging you have been rescued from that kingdom of doubt, fear, and unbelief, you will conquer adversity and experience the fulfillment of your vision.

Remember that God is always working, even when you cannot see all that He is doing. God will reveal what He has been doing at the right time. There will be days when you feel like you have been forsaken. That is the time to praise God and be thankful for what you have already seen accomplished. Abraham patiently waited twenty-five years for the fulfillment of the promise of the son that God had promised him. The Bible says, "Abraham did not waver at the promises of God through unbelief, but was strong in faith, giving glory to God" (Rom. 4:20 NKJV).

Patience is a godly virtue. It simply means to be constant or the same all the time. Keep a positive confession and constant praise coming out of your mouth. REMEMBER, GOD'S DELAYS ARE NOT GOD'S DENIAL. He is faithful and will fulfill every promise. God's love and kindness toward us is greater than any evil the enemy has devised against us. God is a covenant God and will be eternally faithful to keep us and manifest His presence in every circumstance.

"For the mountains shall depart, and the hills be removed; but my kindness shall not depart from you, neither shall the covenant of my peace be removed, says the Lord that has mercy on you" (Isa. 54:10 NKJV).

God has a perfect plan for your life. He is the perfect solution to all your problems and adversities that rise up. We have to trust Him with all our heart knowing He knows what is best for us. "For I know the plans I have for you, declares the Lord, Plans to prosper you and not to harm you, plans to give you hope and a future" (Jer. 29:11 NIV).

At some point in life, we all face hardships. Yours could be physical or emotional. Whatever your difficulty, do not let it discourage you from believing for God's best. Do not allow it to destroy your hope. Choose today to hold on to God's promises. God knows what challenges you face, and He has a way to turn things around for your good. "Let us hold fast the confession of our hope without wavering, for he who promised is faithful" (Heb. 10:23 NKJV).

Get ready for the "best" days of your life.

CHAPTER TEN

DEALING WITH PROBLEMS WITH YOUR VISION

"Never let the problem become an excuse. Always keep the vision and dream before you. Don't allow the problem to cause you to quit."

CHAPTER 10

DEALING WITH PROBLEMS WITH YOUR VISION

"These things I have spoken to you, that in Me you may have peace. In the world you will have tribulation; but be of good cheer, I have overcome the world."
– John 16:33 NKJV

God never said that you would not encounter problems in pursuit of your vision and dream. Every individual will be faced with what we call predicaments. Sometimes we refer to these situations as "being in a pinch." If you are from the South, you are "between a rock and a hard place." Other expressions of a predicament are "you're in a jam," or "in a pickle." I am sure that foreigners trying to decipher our lingo must scratch their head in bewilderment as they hear Americans talking about being "against a wall," "up a tree," "in a corner," "up against it," and "hard pressed."

I recently heard a description of a predicament: A predicament occurs when an attorney who specializes in medical malpractice suits finds himself in need of major surgery. Now that's a predicament!

There are many reasons for predicaments. They could be related to your job and the pressures that are there. It may be a relational issue. No matter what or where it is, when you are in a tight place and you see no way out, that's a predicament.

It may be that right now you find yourself in a predicament. You have begun your pursuit of the vision and dream that God planted in your spirit. You might have made a series of unwise decisions that have placed you "in a pickle." Or, you might find yourself in a predicament through no fault of your own. The enemy could have put up these roadblocks to discourage you from moving forward.

So what is happening? Why is it that when you pursue the vision and dream that negative things happen? Why do insurmountable problems occur to hinder and keep us from fulfilling that vision and dream?

I might ask you what lessons can you learn when you find yourself in a predicament? It might well be the only solution to your predicament is a miracle.

Following God … And Coming to a Dead End

One of the most intriguing accounts in history is the story of Moses, who was called as a baby to deliver the children of Israel out of bondage to fulfill the dream and vision that God had given several hundred years prior. The important thing to recognize here is that the promise and dream was kept alive by the leaders reminding the people about it every day. God did not forget His promise to them. And neither has God forgotten His promise to you, my friend. God is faithful.

Once the orders to leave captivity in Egypt were issued by Moses, all three million of them began their journey. Everything looked good at first. The Egyptians loaded the

Israelites down with gold and silver. They gave them cattle and other animals. Divine provision was evident. It seemed that there would be no hitch in seeing the vision fulfilled.

God had prepared Moses for this moment. Remember how Moses had learned his lessons on the backside of the desert for forty years. He had learned to obey God when specific instructions were issued. So even though God commanded him to march the people toward the Red Sea, it wasn't hard for Moses to obey, to go the direction that seemed contrary to all logic.

This was a sight to behold. Pharaoh had changed his mind. He gathered his mighty army and decided to follow the Israelites and destroy them. God's people could see the dust clouds of the hundreds of chariots and horses pursuing them. The people stood at the banks of the Red Sea with no way to cross. They resorted back to their old nature of grumbling and complaining. Nevertheless, Moses stood up and prophesied to them. He said, "Do not fear! Stand by and see the salvation of the Lord, which he will accomplish for you today; for the Egyptians whom you have seen today, you will never see them again forever. The Lord will fight for you while you keep silent" (Exod. 14:13-14 NKJV).

What a predicament! There was definitely a need for a miracle. And God came through. Of course, there was something God required from Moses. He had to use what was in his hand. What was that? The old rod that he had on the desert—the one God used to reveal His power to Moses when He spoke out of the burning bush. It is not hard to use what you have when you have already seen and proven that

God will use it. Moses lifted his rod out toward the Red Sea as God had commanded.

The miracle began, but it still wasn't evident. The Red Sea did not open up immediately. The Israelites people had to wait all night. But what they saw the next morning was a something to behold. During the night, God caused the east wind to blow across the Red Sea and it parted the water so they could all pass safely to the other side.

Sometimes you might not see all that God is doing in the dark hour that you are facing. Nevertheless, one thing is for sure, He is not sleeping. He is working for your good. All during the night and dark hours God is working and clearing the way. The Scripture says, "Weeping may endure for the night. But joy comes in the morning" (Ps. 30:5 NKJV).

Lessons Learned from Predicaments

More often than not, it takes these predicaments to break lifetime habits. It takes these trying moments to free us from our thought patterns and behaviors that have held us in bondage for years.

We have learned the ways of the world and think as the world does concerning our predicaments. In God's plan for you, these tight places are designed to bring you to the place of "not being conformed to this world, but to be transformed by the renewing of your mind" (Rom.12: 1-3 NKJV).

When we are hemmed in on all sides, the only place to

look is up. The psalmist David wrote, "I will lift up my eyes to the hills, from whence comes my help? My help comes from the Lord, who made heaven and earth" (Ps.121:1-2 NKJV).

Sometimes being under pressure it brings you to the end of yourself. Allow the Lord to do the fighting. He always wins.

Here is a good motto for you to go by when you end up in a predicament:

When I panic, I run,

When I run, I lose,

When I lose, God waits,

When I wait, He fights,

When He fights, He wins,

And when He wins, I learn.

Your vision and dream is important to God. He is aware of every scheme the devil has planned against you. God anticipated it. That is why He has a counterattack prepared against the enemy of your soul. "Vengeance is mine, says the Lord" (Rom. 12:19 NKJV). He will work if you will let Him. He will fight if you will let Him. God is for you and not against you.

Your vision and dream is worth standing and believing

for. Nothing in this world is easy. If it were, everybody would do it. But you can do it, because, "greater is He that is in you than he that is in the world" (1 John 4:4 NKJV).

Problems Come to Cause you to Give Up

The devil does not have the power to stop you from succeeding. All he can do is to create havoc and problems to discourage you from going forward with your vision and dream.

The outcome to your seeing the vision and dream fulfilled is determined how you perceive your problem. It is simply not allowing the problem "to get under your skin." There is something that my older brother always told me when I would relate my vision and dream to him. He would simply say, "Just do it!"

Every problem holds possibilities for you. Your problem today can reveal who you are and uncover a compassion within you that enables you to help others with their problems. What you learn can become a valuable education for others.

Problems will change you. Problems will never leave us the same way they found us. If we react to the problem with fear and confusion, it could be devastating and threaten to destroy the very thing God desires to fulfill in your life.

You can choose what your problem will do to you. You may not have chosen this problem, but you can choose how you will react to it. How are you going to react? Your reaction to the problem is life or death. It can make us tender or tough. It can make you better or bitter. It all depends on you. Never let the problem become an excuse. Always keep the vision and dream before you. Don't allow the problem to cause you to quit.

Your Destiny Can Be Changed

There is a story in the Old Testament about a man named Jabez. His very name speaks of the condition his life was in. Jabez means sorrow, pain, and trouble. His mother called him Jabez because she bore him in sorrow. The Bible does not say what was wrong with Jabez. Was he born with a disease? Or was he simply born in an atmosphere of sorrow, trouble, and heartache? Whatever the case, every time his name was called, it cried out sorrow, trouble, and pain.

"And Jabez was more honorable than his brethren: and his mother called his name Jabez, saying, because I bare him with sorrow." (1 Chron. 4:9 KJV)

Has the enemy convinced you that your destiny in life is to suffer pain and always experience defeat? Have you thrown up your hands in surrender to the circumstances and resigned yourself to the fact that nothing else can be done about your situation?

Multitudes of people around the world who once lived in a hopeless situation have come to the revelation of God's Word and found that rising up out of the dunghill and grasping hold of the promises of God could change their lives eternally.

Jabez was in the same position as many of you are today. It seemed that each day was filled with more heartache and sorrow. He is convinced there is nothing better for him. He has confined himself to these chains of defeat. Many of you who are reading this book are chained to your past. You are confined within the walls of deceit that imprison your spirit and you cannot see beyond them, because the enemy has blinded your spiritual eyes. Your dream and vision is confined because you are the deciding vote on whether you break free or not.

It is possible that Jabez was able to hear the prophet of God speak about the goodness of God, or perhaps he heard the prophet minister on "Is there anything too hard for God?" When Jabez could see God's truth, he began to break free from the lies of the devil that had contained him. He denied the enemy the power to control his thinking and keep him living in the darkness of sickness and bondage.

Jabez began to call upon the God of mercy and love. He prayed a prayer that moved God to bless him. Listen to what he prayed. "And Jabez called on the God of Israel, saying, 'Oh that you would bless me indeed, and enlarge my coast, and that your hand would be with me, and that you would keep me from evil, that it would not grieve me!' And God granted him that which he requested" (1 Chron. 4:10 NKJV).

Jabez wanted the blessing of God, but he desired more. He wanted to be loosed and freed. He wanted God to enlarge his coast, his boundaries. He was saying, "Deliver me from these confining walls of fear and defeat. I want all the barriers broken down. I want to live a life with no limitations.

God granted him what he requested.

Jabez also requested that God would keep him from evil. He wanted to live a life pleasing to the Lord. He wanted all evidence of past defeat and pain to be gone.

My friend, God is waiting for you to cry out to Him as Jabez did. You have to come to the place that you are tired of being sick and tired. You have to desire the abundant provisions that God has reserved for you. Call upon God today. He wants to deliver you from these predicaments and problems that have plagued you and your family for these many years.

Those walls of containment are going to crumble. The doors of that prison are going to be kicked open. You will begin to look up and see a new horizon with no limits in your life. Your vision and dream will have more than sufficient resources. Your mind will be renewed with the revelation of the Word of God. You will begin to demonstrate to the world that you live in a new kingdom where King Jesus rules.

The Vision Will Speak

Waiting on God can become a very exhausting thing when we allow predicaments and problems to influence our thoughts. These negative things do not disprove God's promises, nor do they stop the promise of God from being fulfilled. If anything, you should learn from these distractions that God's presence is with you regardless of where you are what is happening all around you. He will never leave you or forsake you. He has promised to be with you until the end. He also has garrisoned His angels of protection and provision around you to minister to you because you are an heir of salvation. (See Hebrews 1:14.)

There is an appointed time for your vision and dream. Don't hurry the process of the growth and development of that dream seed. When it is time for the manifestation, it will happen. It will speak volumes at the end and it will not lie. The whole world will know that God has performed His will in your life. The divine favor of God will show up in everything you do.

The key is for you is to learn to wait, even though it looks like it tarries. It will surely come. It will truly happen. You will rejoice because you have learned to live in faith.

"For the vision is yet for an appointed time, but at the end it will speak, and it will not lie. Even though it tarries, wait for it; because it will surely come and not tarry." Habakkuk 2:3

CHAPTER ELEVEN

DREAM KILLERS

"The assurance that you have as a believer knows that the enemy cannot stop the dream seed, which God put deep in your spirit, from bursting forth and coming to its full potential."

CHAPTER 11

DREAM KILLERS

"For assuredly, I say to you, whoever says to this mountain, 'Be removed and be cast into the sea,' and does not doubt in his heart, but believes that those things he says will be done, he will have whatever he says. "
– Mark 11:23 NKJV

Do you have a dream inside you? Do you carry it within you as a soon-to-be-mom carries a child in her womb? Just as a baby takes time to develop, it takes time for dreams to become reality. It takes you "seeing" as God sees you and "seeing" your dream coming to pass. Notice carefully the three-letter word "see." Seeing is an internal attitude. Seeing is vision. Seeing is a dream that possesses your mind. Seeing is what gives motivation to propel us forward into what God has in store for each one of us.

Joseph had a dream within him. I am convinced its power and clarity kept him up at night. As clearly as he could see the stars in the sky, he could see what was inside him. It was a force that kept him alive. Abraham had a dream of possessing all that God had promised him he would possess. Caleb had a dream. He has seen a parcel of land he claimed for himself. He would not be denied having the access to what he knew would someday be his. Nehemiah had a dream of having walls built back around Jerusalem, the city he loved with all his heart, protecting the people he so cared about. Esther had a dream of preserving the Jews in her land from a ruthless and evil edict. If you take the time to go through the Word of God, you will find many more people who dreamed big dreams inside themselves.

Children dream big. Ask any child what he or she want to be when they grow up and you will get myriad answers. A doctor, lawyer, police officer, firefighter, princess, king, teacher. The list is endless. A child possesses a dream within, so that while they play, they live out the dreams before our eyes. Never once, do you hear a child, when asked what he or she wants to be, say loser, misfit, no good, poor, wretched, and miserable. Why? Their dreams keep them alive. On the inside, this powerful force flows forth within them providing motivation to reach toward that which they can see inside their own heart and mind.

I was thinking in my spirit about things that destroy our dreams. I call them "Dream Killers." They take away our motivation, our drive, our enthusiasm, our hope, our calling. Pardon me if this word bothers you, but I *hate* dream killers. Permit me to list just a few that resonate within my spirit today.

1. **Negative people** are dream killers. They see a glass half empty instead of half full. They tell us it cannot be done. They extinguish the flame burning inside our hearts. You've met these people at least once in your life. They refuse to dream; therefore, it bothers them to be around people who dare to dream. They do everything in their power to hold us back. Joseph's bothers were a negative bunch. And as

we learned from his story, it is best not to tell *everyone* what is on the inside of your life.

2. **Jealousy** is a dream killer. There is not one of us who, at one time or another, has not fought against this enemy. Solomon, with the wisdom of heaven alive inside of himself wrote, "…jealousy is as cruel as the grave…" (Song of Sol. 8:6 KJV).

3. **Fear** is a dream killer. So powerful is this enemy that it keeps many of God's people in bondage, unable to move forward under the mandate of heaven. Fear causes us to live from the outside inward instead of the reverse. It causes our legs to feel heavy, like weights that cannot be picked up. It extinguishes that inner flame that provides the motivation to pursue what we have been dreaming.

4. **Doubt** is a dream killer. If the verse is not marked in your Bible, or if you do not know what it says, get a New Testament, and find Mark 11:23. Underline the verse. Write it on the tablet of your mind. Put it on a 3X5 card and tape it to the mirror in your bathroom. Let the words become life to your spirit-man. Jesus promised that whatever we could dream of and begin to say with our mouth, we could have, IF this dream killer was not allowed to enter in. .

I have no way of knowing what dream you see inside your life at this very moment. Whatever God has birthed in your life, it is time to allow it to come to fruition. Silence the critics in your life. Shut your ears to those people who want you to fail. Refuse to be bound with what others are saying about you and your dream. I am convinced that God is looking for dreamers to rise from within the body of Christ —people who will see what others refuse to see and will do what others refuse to do. It is time to dream and dream big. This is our hour. The sky is the limit. I challenge you today that if your dreams have been dormant, it is time for them to be stirred. Don't allow dream killers to take from you what God has birthed within you. It does not matter how long it takes to see the results. Never give up on your dreams. God is for you and there is nothing or no one who can be against you.

> ***It is time to dream and dream big because our God is a BIG God!***

God wants you to allow His peace to rule your heart. One thing that will get you off track is lack of peace. Sometimes you have to get somewhere alone with God and bask in His presence and have the assurance that He has not left you but is guiding each step.

Have you ever stepped out in faith to do what God has put in your heart to fulfill? There is a sense of expectancy. You have joy that is unparalleled to any joy that you have experienced. Peace beyond measure fills your heart and mind, knowing that the God that leads also provides. Your faith level reaches a utopia. In your mind, there is nothing that is going to stop God's plan for your life.

Then one day the emotional feelings are not present. You stand there assessing the situation. Questions begin to swarm your thought pattern: Did I do the right thing? What have I done? What if I missed God on this decision?

This is a natural reaction that every one of us has at one time or another. It is a safety feature that God has programmed into our spirits to protect us from pride and destruction. You see, God wants you to know and feel that you are nothing without Him. Our strength alone will not enable us to accomplish this great goal and dream that God has birthed in our spirit. It is bigger than we are. In fact, it will take a miracle to see it come to fruition.

Just recently, God spoke to my spirit concerning something that He wanted for my life. I was exuberant with joy and anticipation of obeying every command. I moved in faith and began to proceed with the actions that will propel me to the next level of the ministry God is orchestrating. Peace that I have experienced on each major event in my life was there. I was eager to do each thing God required. I obeyed and was ready to move in any direction that God desired.

A couple of days had passed since I obeyed, and I was anticipating the finalization of this part of my dream and vision. Then out of nowhere, the thoughts began to invade my mind. "What have I done? Did I do the right thing?" Troubled thoughts were there where peace had ruled the day before.

I got in my van and drove about eight miles to a "Prayer Garden" that a church has built for people to sit or walk and commune with the Lord. I found myself alone there. I sat on a bench overlooking a beautiful pond with a cross standing in the middle. The waterspouts were shooting water upward with the most peaceful sound, which seemed to overtake the questions that were crowding my mind. The peace of God that passes all understanding soothed my mind and spirit. It was as if God sedated me and began to speak to my heart. I remembered His words of comfort: "Yes, you can do all things through My Son Jesus Christ.. You are more than a conqueror. I am with you and will never leave you. All things are possible to him that believes." All at once, I found myself resting and did not realize until forty-five minutes later that I had rested and slept with the promises of God in my thoughts.

When I awoke, I went over to a plaque that was on the path in front of the bench where I had been resting. The plaque had a Scripture inscribed on it. "Be still and know that I am God: I will be exalted among the heathen, I will be exalted in the earth. The Lord of Hosts is with us; the God of Jacob is our refuge" (Ps. 46:10-11 KJV).

I left that prayer garden with assurance in my heart that God is in control of my life. He is with me and guiding each step that I take. I learned to be still and know that He is God.

The assurance that you have as a believer knows that the enemy cannot stop the dream seed, which God put deep in your spirit, from bursting forth and coming to its full potential. The only thing the enemy can try to do is to influence your mind with thoughts of confusion and anxiety. The devil has no control over your thoughts and mind as long as you keep your mind stayed on the Lord and His promises. The Scripture says, "You will keep him in perfect peace whose mind is stayed on you; because he trusts in you"

(Isa. 26:3 NKJV)

My friend, you are too close to seeing your vision and dream fulfilled to allow these dream killers to stop you in your tracks. Remember that God is not playing games with you. He desires for you to be filled with joy in knowing you found His purpose that He designed for your life before you were born. You are the "apple of His eye" and He as your Father will do everything that is necessary to see it all happen for you. Our Father is glorified through your success in life and the fulfillment of the vision and dream that is exclusively yours.

I read this quote one day and it ministered to my heart:

> ***Only God can turn a mess into a message, a test into a testimony, a trial into a triumph, a victim into a victory.***

This is all so true. You are born to triumph over every obstacle the enemy puts in front of you. You are a conqueror. The reward belongs to you. Take it and live a life that brings all glory to God.

CHAPTER TWELVE

ENLARGING YOUR VISION

"There is no limit to what God can do. There is no limit to what you can do for the Lord. Your faith will carry you to higher heights."

CHAPTER TWELVE

ENLARGING YOUR VISION

"For every beast of the forest are mine,
and the cattle on a thousand hills."
– Psalm 50:10 NKJV

God has already anticipated all that is needed to complete the dream and vision that He birthed within your spirit. He has supplied all the provisions before you ever need them. The Apostle Paul wrote, "and this He said although His works had been completed and prepared {and waiting for all who would believe} from the foundation of the world" (Heb. 4:3b AMP).

There is an old saying, "which came first, the air that we breathe, or the lungs to breathe in the air?" The provisions for our physical body were here before we ever needed them. The provisions for our financial needs were here before we ever had need of them. God owns all the gold, silver, and all ores in the earth. He owns every beast of the forest and all the cattle on a thousand hills. (One preacher said he owns all the taters underneath the ground, too.)

As you read the Scriptures of God's abundant provision, you understand that everything that is necessary for the vision and dream that He gave you is available. There are no limitations on what you can obtain to fulfill your purpose in life.

Develop the Proper Attitude

Attitude is an important element in the success and fulfillment of your dream and vision. Attitude determines your altitude. It will make you or break you. A positive attitude is essential in order for everything to flow smoothly. You need an "I can" attitude. You cannot look at the situation as impossible. Remember, God already anticipated the obstacles that would confront you today. He already has an abundant supply of courage and inner strength for you to overcome every negative thing. You are what you think. You cannot go by the natural. You walk by faith, not being moved by what you see. There is no limit to what you can do. Your faith will carry you to higher heights.

The definition of the word "attitude" is "a feeling of emotion toward something. It is your mental position with regard to a fact or state of circumstances." An attitude could be defined as "a position that you take as a result of your reaction to a situation."

Your attitude determines whether your vision and dream will be fulfilled. Your response to a situation will cause you to either have a breakthrough or fall short of seeing the completion of the vision and dream. If your spirit is weak, even the smallest thing that the enemy throws at you will cause you to react negatively to the problem instead of acting with faith, allowing God to move for you and through you.

An attitude of fear and an "I can't" attitude exhaust you mentally and physically. When you are tired, you want to stop pressing forward. Your zeal has vanished. You just do not have the desire to get up and do what God knows you can do.

As you begin to see that God has provided everything that you need to fulfill your vision, you will sense a surge of spiritual energy and will experience a peace that settles your mind and spirit. That peace is the peace of God that passes all understanding. This peace will give you that spiritual boost you need and the emotional stamina to endure.

There is no limit to what God can do.
There is no limit to what you can do for the Lord
Your faith will carry you to higher heights.

Expand Your Boundaries

Are you content with where you are right now? Do you see anything better than what you are and what you have in your hand at this moment? What are you expecting to happen in your life?

You have to be willing to change your level of expectancy. The only way to change the level of expectation that you have is to change your way of thinking. The mind is the arena where the battle rages, where the enemy of your soul sows seeds of fear and unworthiness, hoping that you will see yourself as a nobody and unworthy of the best that God has already provided for you.

The Apostle Paul wrote to the church at Rome, encouraging the people not to be conformed to the world. In other words, do not allow the world system and its way of thinking rule over the Word of God and His plans for you. Rather, be transformed or changed by renewing your mind to God's thoughts toward you so that you will know that good and perfect will of God for you and your vision.

"And do not be conformed to this world but be transformed by the renewing of your mind that you may prove what is that good, and acceptable, and perfect will of God." (Rom. 12:2 NKJV)

The mind can keep you imprisoned and your memory locked into the past. Your past should never dictate your future. There is one thing that God has put in each of us and that is the power to change. You can change your way of thinking. You can change your actions and habits of the past. You are not chained to your past. Allowing the past to rule and dominate your life causes you live with limitations. If you will change your thinking, God will change your life.

Come Into Your Land of Promise

After forty years of wandering in circles and not entering into the land that God had given them, God finally allowed the Israelites to move forward into the land of promise. Prior to their exodus from Egypt, they had lived in a slave camp. They had been in bondage there for four hundred years. They had learned to do without and subject themselves to their captors.

The children of Israel were filled with ecstasy and joy when they were set free from the physical slave camp. They were singing songs of deliverance and dancing as they went on their journey. They were free from the bondage of Egypt, but they had a hard time getting Egypt out of their thinking. They had been programmed to think as slaves. So, God had them wait for their promised prophecy. It is the same with many people today. They have been set free from the power of the enemy, but their mind is still programmed to think as one who is defeated.

I have counseled women who have come out of an abusive relationship. They are no longer in a position to be hurt or abused, but their mind keeps them cowered down in their spirit. They don't see themselves as being free and having a new start in life. Many individuals have failed in life with businesses and lost everything they had. Now they cannot get up and get going again because the past failures always haunt their memory.

God is saying that it's time to move forward, let go of past hurts, pain, or failures. It's time to believe God for bigger things. But we have to change our thinking and begin to think the thoughts of God and speak them from our lips.

The time had finally come for the children of Israel to enter into the land God had provided. The land flowed with milk and honey. All the provisions that were necessary were already there. Now the land was theirs, but they had to do what was necessary to march forward and possess it. God had led them up to the bank of the Jordan River. God had babysat the Children of Israel for eighty years. Now it was time for them to mature and grow up. Moses had died and now Joshua was the leader whom Moses had mentored to take over. Joshua had been one of the twelve men who spied out the land. Joshua and Caleb came back with a good report stating that it was just as God said it would be. He saw the glass half-full.

God gave instructions to the new leader, Joshua, after the death of Moses. God assured him that as He was with Moses, He would be with him. Joshua gave the command to move forward, as God has instructed. The word they received that day was to arise and go forward over the Jordan River into the land that God had given them. The exhortation they received that day was one of victory. They were told that they were establishing their boundaries for their inheritance. Every place that the soles of their feet would tread upon, God had given it to them. The borders for them were well defined. A new vast territory now belonged to them.

"Now therefore arise, and go over this Jordan, you and all this people, to the land which I am giving to them. Every place that the sole of your foot will tread upon I have given you as I said to Moses." (Josh. 1:2-3 NKJV)

You are about to enter a new, fresh era of your life. No matter what you have gone through in the past, no matter how many setbacks you have suffered, today is a new day. God wants to do a new thing in your life. Get ready to step into your new territory. There is no limit to what God can do in your life. You are the deciding factor. How far do you want to penetrate into the new land that God has opened up to you? It is yours. That vision and dream that God birthed in you is ready to be fulfilled. Start claiming your territory by putting your foot down and proclaiming that it is yours.

You can become content with where you are and what you have or you can decide today that the vision and dream you hold came from God and you will do what is necessary to see it come to pass. The Bible says in the book of Isaiah for you "to enlarge the place of your tent and to stretch out the curtains of your dwellings. Do not spare; lengthen your cords and strengthen your stakes. For you shall expand to the right hand and the left" (Isa. 54:2-3 NKJV).

When God programmed that vision and dream within you, He desired that it be fruitful. Start now! Walk in faith and begin to stake out the new territory. Take off all the limits and don't leave any room for doubt and fear to hinder your progress. Strengthen the stakes that are the stability of your dream and vision. The stake of faith needs to be driven deep, because faith is the very nature of a winner. The stake of fellowship with the Lord Himself is vital to your spiritual growth and maturity. This where you learn to live in the presence of the Lord and where His strength becomes your strength.

Yes, this is a brand new day for you! You will begin to see God accelerate the plans that he designed for you. People will see the favor of God in your life. And God will be glorified in this earth by your vision and dream becoming a reality.

CONCLUSION

IT IS NEVER TOO LATE

CONCLUSION

IT'S NEVER TOO LATE

Jesus was on a journey with His disciples. They were a few days from Bethany, where a close friend, Lazarus, lived with his sisters, Martha and Mary. Lazarus became seriously ill, so Mary sent word to Jesus to hurry and come and lay hands on her brother and heal him.

When Jesus received this urgent message, He tarried four more days where he was. The disciples did not understand His actions because Lazarus was Jesus' best friend. After a few days, Jesus decided to go to Bethany. But in the meantime, Lazarus had died and was buried.

When they were a short distance from the house, Martha ran to meet Jesus. When she got there, she frantically cried and said that if he had been there, Lazarus would not have died. Jesus replied, "Your brother will rise again ... I am the resurrection and the life ... If you will believe you will see the glory of God" (John 11:23,25,40 NKJV).

When they got to the tomb, Jesus asked Martha to have the stone rolled away. Martha again became frantic and said, "Did you not hear me on the road? Lazarus is dead and he stinks by now because it has been four days." Jesus replied, "Did I not tell you that if you would believe you would see the glory of God revealed today, because I am the resurrection and the life?"

They rolled the stone away. Jesus stood at the opening of the tomb and commanded Lazarus to come forth. Lazarus immediately came bounding out of the tomb, still wrapped in his grave clothes. Jesus told the people to loose him and let him go.

My friend, I am here to tell you that it does not matter how long your dream or vision has been buried. God has not changed His mind concerning you or the purpose He has for your life. Today, God wants you to roll that stone away from the opening of your heart and let Him speak the words "Come forth!" to that dream and vision. It does not matter if it comes forth all wrapped and in bondage. God has assigned people in your life to help take the grave clothes off and assist you with your vision and dream. They are already positioned to help fulfill this dream.

Don't be intimidated by the stone that has been rolled over the entrance to your dream's tomb. Move forward and roll it back. God wants to reveal His glory to you. He wants to bring back to life the dreams and visions that you have allowed to die.

That spark of hope that you are sensing right now is the "truth" of the Word of God that is liberating your mind and spirit from the bonds of your present circumstances. For the first time, many of you are seeing yourself as God sees you. He sees you as a winner. He sees you as a conqueror over the obstacles that have hindered you from becoming all that He has designed for you to become.

The next step for you is to shake off the grave cloths that have tied you down. Rise up and begin this new journey of faith. Fulfill that dream and vision that has been in you before you were conceived. Each day from this time forth will become a testimony of the faithfulness of God and His supernatural power that enables you to fulfill that vision.

I want to take this opportunity and encourage you to get ready. The greatest joy you have ever experienced is about to explode in your spirit. There is nothing more exhilarating than to be able to lie down at night knowing that you have pleased God and are fulfilling His vision for your life.

Note from the Author:

Every person has a “story” to tell about how his or her dream and vision has developed. Please write me and share the results of the revelation from this book that inspired you to move into a new realm of faith. I pray for you now that God will open your eyes of understanding and enlighten you to His perfect will for your life. I pray that the fruit of your labor will flourish as you step out on the promises of God so the special dream and vision that is unique to you will be fulfilled.

Clarence Dalrymple
Clarence@living-faith-ministries.com

ABOUT THE AUTHOR

CLARENCE DALRYMPLE

Rev. Clarence Dalrymple is known as one of the Fathers of the Faith message. He is the founder of Living Faith Ministries International. Inc. which was established in 1986. This ministry has taken Clarence to many countries of the world where he conducts crusades and Pastor and Leadership Conferences. He also is an author.

His latest books are "The Dream Seed - God's Blueprint within You" and "Transformed By The Desert Experience - Redefining Your Call and Refining Your Character."

Clarence Dalrymple has been in full time ministry since 1965. After graduation from high school he conducted youth revivals and traveled with his dad, Dr. W.C. Dalrymple, assisting him with tent revivals throughout the Southwestern part of the United States. In 1966 Clarence made the decision to attended Southern Bible College in Houston, Texas. After his graduation from college he and his family began attending Lakewood Church in Houston, Texas where Dr. John Osteen was the pastor. There he became the associate pastor for four years. As Clarence's style of preaching and teaching developed, it has been evident that his method of ministry has blessed many people through the years.

Clarence brings clarity to the wisdom of God through his preaching and teaching. Throughout the years of his ministry many lives have been changed and transformed through his ministering the power of the Word of God.

In 2012 he relocated Living Faith Ministries International, Inc. to New England after receiving a Word from the Lord. Clarence feels that The New Awakening is going to be the beginning of revival that will spread throughout the United States.

Clarence's desire is for everyone to experience the presence of God and receive divine revelation of His Word so that people know their worth and experience the goodness of God's Covenant promises.

For a listing of all materials by Clarence Dalrymple,
go to *www.living-faith-ministries.com*

or,

Write and request at:

Living Faith Ministries International, Inc.,
P.O. Box 292
Conroe, TX 77305-0292